Level 1 Bookkeeping Skills

for OCR QCF Level 1 Award in Bookkeeping Skills (Manual)

Michael Fardon

Sheila Robinson

osborne
BOOKS

Published by Osborne Books Limited
Unit 1B Everoak Estate
Bromyard Road
Worcester WR2 5HP
Tel 01905 748071
Email books@osbornebooks.co.uk
Website www.osbornebooks.co.uk

Design by Richard Holt

Printed by CPI Antony Rowe Limited, Chippenham

British Library Cataloguing in Publication Data
A catalogue record for this book is available from the British Library

ISBN 978 1905777 631

CONTENTS

ACKNOWLEDGEMENTS

The authors wish to thank the following for their help with the reading and production of this book: Maz Loton, Jon Moore, Cathy Turner and Lynn Watkins. The publisher is very grateful to the staff at OCR who have provided invaluable advice and support during the course of this project.

THE AUTHORS

Michael Fardon has extensive teaching experience of a wide range of banking, business and accountancy courses at Worcester College of Technology. He now specialises in writing business and financial texts and is General Editor at Osborne Books. He is also an educational consultant and has worked extensively in the areas of vocational business curriculum development.

Sheila Robinson worked for a firm of accountants before gaining extensive teaching experience at Stockport College of Higher and Further Education, where, as Senior Lecturer, she taught on accounting and management courses. Sheila is a well-established author of bookkeeping and accountancy books and is a former Council Member of the Association of Accounting Technicians.

INTRODUCTION

the textbook

Level 1 Bookkeeping Skills has been written as a practical guide for students studying the QCF-based units of the OCR Level 1 Award in Bookkeeping Skills, which deals with manual bookkeeping:

Unit M1   Preparing & processing bookkeeping documents

Unit M2   Recording credit transactions

Unit M3   Making & receiving payments

Unit M4   Recording receipts and payments

Unit M5   Maintaining petty cash records

The book assumes no previous knowledge of bookkeeping and is an ideal introduction for people who are interested in preparing for a job in bookkeeping, or who are already working in a bookkeeping role.

The text of *Level 1 Bookkeeping Skills* contains:

* clear and practical explanations
* step-by-step Case Studies
* Key Terms and Chapter Summaries for revision
* practical Student Activities, many with answers at the back of the book, based on the format of the OCR assessments

completing accounts and documents

A large part of the OCR course involves the completion of documents. To help with this, Osborne Books has printed suitable blank financial documents in a 'document bank' at the end of the book. Tutors and students are welcome to photocopy these, as indicated in the text. Alternatively, this photocopiable material is available as a free download from the Resources section of the Osborne Books website: www.osbornebooks.co.uk

online Tutor Resources

Osborne Books website (www.osbornebooks.co.uk) contains tutor resources (financial documents and answers to selected questions) in a password-protected area. This material is available to tutors who have adopted this textbook for student use. To apply for access to this tutor resource material please complete the online application form at www.osbornebooks.co.uk.

OCR ASSESSMENT CRITERIA MAPPING

Unit M4: Recording receipts and payments

Unit M5: Maintaining petty cash records

1 Processing documents for credit sales

what this chapter covers . . .

This chapter:

- explains what 'credit sales' means – ie 'sell now and be paid later'

- describes the documents involved when a credit sale is made; these include:
  - the purchase order – issued by the buyer ordering goods and services
  - the price list – which sets out the price of what is being ordered
  - the sales invoice – issued by the seller, setting out the details of the transaction, including the price charged, any discounts, Value Added Tax, and the total amount due

- explains the function of the sales credit note and the goods returned note – documents completed when goods are sent back to the seller for a refund

- describes how invoices and credit notes are accurately completed with details of the customer and product codes

OCR assessment criteria covered

Unit M1: Preparing and processing bookkeeping documents

1.1 Prepare sales invoices and sales credit notes from source documents

1.2 Calculate relevant sales tax (eg VAT) and check it has been applied accurately

1.3 Code sales invoices and credit notes

CREDIT SALES

manual and computerised bookkeeping

In your studies of bookkeeping you will deal with a number of financial documents which are used at various stages of the buying and selling process. Nowadays these documents are often produced on a computer, using software such as Sage. In this book and in your studies of manual (hand-written) bookkeeping, however, you will deal with paper-based records and documents. In doing this you will be able to learn and understand more easily the principles and processes involved.

cash and credit sales – some definitions

When a business sells goods and services, it can:

- *either* ask for payment straightaway; this arrangement is known as a **cash sale** and payment can be made using actual cash, or a debit or credit card

- *or* it can allow the person or business buying the goods or services to pay on credit – this means that the buyer will pay at an agreed later date, often by cheque or bank transfer; this arrangement is known as a **credit sale**

This chapter will explain the processes and documents involved when a business sells **on credit**.

credit sales – a summary of the documents used

The buyer of the goods and services will often use a **purchase order** which is sent to the seller. This document sets out the details of the goods or services required and, in many cases, the advertised price.

The central document involved in a credit sale is the **sales invoice** prepared by the seller for the buyer. The sales invoice sets out the details of the goods sold, the price charged and the time allowed for the buyer to pay the due amount.

Before preparing the sales invoice the seller will check an up-to-date **price list** which will ensure that the correct price is charged.

The goods sold will then be sent out with a **delivery note** which sets out the details of the goods and the delivery method.

If the goods sent out are found to be faulty or incorrect they will be returned to the seller by the buyer accompanied by a **goods returned note** which will list the goods and state what the problem is. As this return of goods will then reduce the amount owed by the buyer, the seller will need to send to the buyer a **credit note** which will set out the reduction in the amount owing.

the 'flow of documents'

This 'flow of documents' between the seller and the buyer is shown in the diagram below. Note how a different type of document is required at each stage of the process.

Also note that the return of goods and the issue of a goods returned note and a credit note only occurs when there is a problem with the goods. Normally once an invoice is issued the buyer will settle up on the due date and there will be no need for any adjustment in the amount owed.

Study the diagram below carefully and then read the detailed descriptions of the individual financial documents in the pages which follow.

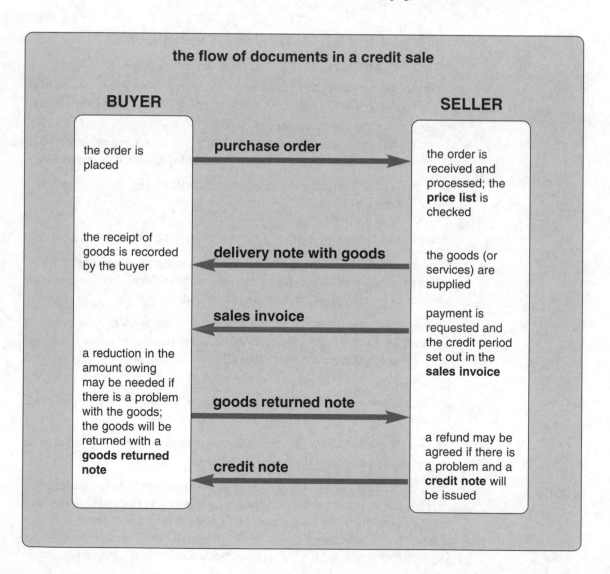

the flow of documents in a credit sale

BUYER

SELLER

the order is placed

purchase order →

the order is received and processed; the **price list** is checked

the receipt of goods is recorded by the buyer

← **delivery note with goods**

the goods (or services) are supplied

← **sales invoice**

payment is requested and the credit period set out in the **sales invoice**

a reduction in the amount owing may be needed if there is a problem with the goods; the goods will be returned with a **goods returned note**

goods returned note →

← **credit note**

a refund may be agreed if there is a problem and a **credit note** will be issued

DOCUMENTS FOR CREDIT SALES – A CASE STUDY

To illustrate the format of the financial documents and the part that they play in the buying and selling process we will track the sale (and return) of some stationery items. There are two businesses involved:

- Presto Supplies, the seller – a stationery wholesaler
- Wyvern Stationery, the buyer – a small stationery business

Be clear in your mind which business is the seller and which is the buyer. In this chapter we will concentrate on the process from the point of view of the seller.

the seller receives a purchase order

Wyvern Stationery wants to buy some photocopier paper and pencils for use in the office. The business compares different supplier catalogues and websites for prices and chooses Presto Supplies. Wyvern Stationery then completes a **purchase order** which it sends to Presto Supplies.

Study the details of the document shown below. Note the following details:

- the product codes CP5R and PHB50 (which are taken from the Presto Supplies price list – see next page)
- the purchase order number 10450 which identifies the order
- the prices taken from the price list

PURCHASE ORDER		Wyvern Stationery
		141, Bell Lane, Wyvern **WY1 4DB**
		Tel 01907 761234 Fax 01907 761987
		Email info@wyvernstationery.co.uk
		VAT REG GB 0745 8383 56

supplier
Presto Supplies
18 Fencote Road
Worcester
WR2 6HY

purchase order no	10450
date	9 December 2011

product code	quantity	description
CP5R	2	A4 Alba copy paper (2500 pack) @ £22.00
PHB50	1	HB Pencils (50 pack) @ £3.45

Presto Supplies checks the price list

When the purchase order is received by Presto Supplies, the accounts staff will need to check that:

• the prices for the copy paper and pencils on the purchase order are up-to-date and can reliably be used on the **sales invoice** which they will have to prepare and send to Wyvern Stationery

• the product codes on the purchase order are correct – CP5R and PHB50

They can do this checking by comparing the purchase order against their **price list** which may be in paper format, or available on a computer screen. The copy paper and pencils are highlighted in the illustration below.

PRESTO SUPPLIES: PRICE LIST (extract)		
Product code	Description	Price (£)
CP1R	A4 Alba copy paper (250 pack)	2.95
CP5R	A4 Alba copy paper (2500 pack)	22.00
LAB01	1-Line Permanent Labels, white (6000 pack)	11.95
C4WSS	C4 Self-seal envelopes, white (250 pack)	24.00
C4WPL	C4 Plain envelopes, manilla, gummed (50 pack)	4.95
DLWSS	DL Self-seal envelopes, white (100 pack)	3.95
C4WPL	DL Plain envelopes, white, gummed (100 pack)	2.95
RBBU5	AlbaGel Rollerball, blue (5 pack)	4.95
RBBK5	AlbaGel Rollerball, black (5 pack)	4.95
RBRD5	AlbaGel Rollerball, red (5 pack)	4.95
PHB50	HB Pencils (50 pack)	3.45
PHBE24	HB Pencils with eraser (24 pack)	5.95
SNY12	Sticky Notes, 76x76mm, yellow (12 pack)	9.95
SNC6	Sticky Notes, 76x76mm, mixed colours (6 pack)	6.95
BFG	Senator foolscap box file, green	2.95
RBBK	2-ring PVC binder, A4, black	1.20
SFA4G	A4 suspension files, green (50 pack)	15.00
WPUM	Unmounted wall planner	4.95

When these details have been checked and found to be correct the **sales invoice** can then be prepared. This is explained on the next page.

INVOICE

An **invoice** is a financial document which is sent by the seller of goods or services to a buyer. When an invoice is issued, normally the goods or services have been sold **on credit**. This means that the goods or services will be paid for at a later date. The Presto Supplies invoice is illustrated and explained in full on the next two pages. An invoice will normally show:

- **details** (name and address) of the seller and buyer
- the **date** of the invoice and its unique **number**
- **details** of the goods or services that have been sold
  - how many items, a description of what they are and their **price**
- the amount due after deduction of any discount
  - a discount is a percentage reduction in the price, for example
    20% trade discount on goods costing £100 is £100 x 20/100
    = a £20 reduction in price
- **VAT** (Value Added Tax) charged on the goods
  - VAT is a government tax which is charged at a set percentage of the invoice total
- the **time period** allowed before payment has to be made
  - a period within 30 days of the invoice date is an example

sales invoices and supplier invoices – a note

A **sales invoice** is an invoice issued by a business which sells goods and services. When you deal with a business situation in your studies and in the exam, you need to think about a sales invoice as the document which is **issued by you**. This is the situation covered in this chapter. Often in the exam the seller has two or more types of product and there is no trade discount involved, although in practice a trade discount may be deducted.

A **supplier invoice** is an invoice received by a business which has bought goods and services from a supplier. When you deal with a business situation in an exam you need to think about a supplier invoice as the document which is **received by you** from someone else. Supplier invoices are dealt with in the next chapter.

Remember that supplier and sales invoices are **not** different formats of invoice; they are the same document with a different description - 'supplier' and 'sales' – depending on who you are in the transaction: the purchaser or the seller. In this chapter you are the seller and so it is a **sales invoice**.

Now study the sales invoice shown and explained on the next two pages.

the **name**, **address** and **contact details** of the **seller**

reference details include:

- the **invoice** number
- the reference number of the **purchase order** (so that the invoice can be 'tied up' with the order by the buyer)
- the **date** of the **invo**ice – this is important for working out when the invoice has to be paid by the buyer (see **terms** below)

the **name** and **address** of the **buyer (customer)**

columns for:

- the **quantity** of each item
- the **product code** of each item
- the **description** of each item
- the **unit price** – how much a single item costs
- the **total** is the quantity multiplied by the unit price for each item (eg 2 x £22 = £44.00)

- the **sub-total** is the total of the items in the total column above it and is used as the basis figure for working out the VAT
- the **VAT @ 20%** is the sub-total multiplied by the VAT percentage (£47.45 x 20% = £9.49)
- the **invoice total** is the sub-total plus the VAT (£47.45 + £9.49 = £56.94); this is the total amount charged to the buyer for the items on the invoice

the **terms** of an invoice set out **when the invoice has to be paid** – for example 'Net 30 days' means that the invoice has to be paid within 30 days of the invoice date

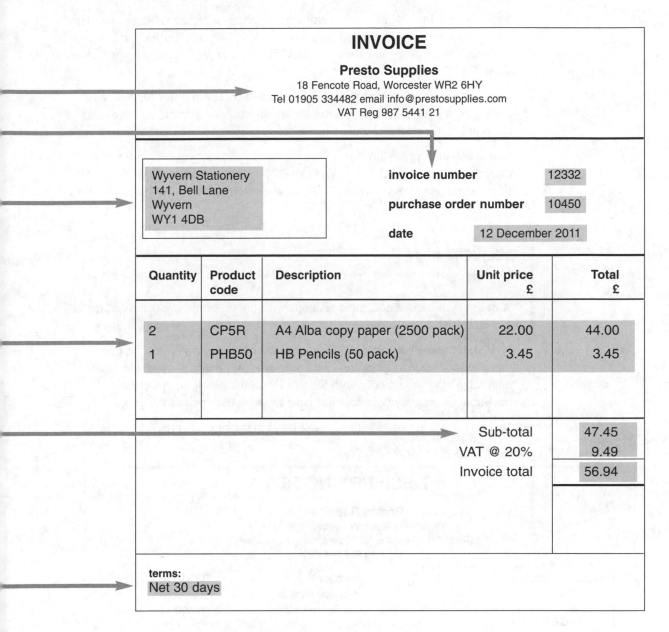

INVOICE

Presto Supplies
18 Fencote Road, Worcester WR2 6HY
Tel 01905 334482 email info@prestosupplies.com
VAT Reg 987 5441 21

Wyvern Stationery
141, Bell Lane
Wyvern
WY1 4DB

invoice number	12332
purchase order number	10450
date	12 December 2011

Quantity	Product code	Description	Unit price £	Total £
2	CP5R	A4 Alba copy paper (2500 pack)	22.00	44.00
1	PHB50	HB Pencils (50 pack)	3.45	3.45
		Sub-total		47.45
		VAT @ 20%		9.49
		Invoice total		56.94

terms:
Net 30 days

issuing the sales invoice

The invoice which has been issued by Presto Supplies in response to the order from Wyvern stationery is shown above. The information which has a grey background has been added by Presto Supplies. Explanations of the various details are on the opposite page. Read them through carefully, paying special attention to the calculations involved. Further notes about VAT on invoices are set out on the next page.

Value Added Tax (VAT)

Value Added Tax (VAT) is a Government tax charged on the selling price of goods and services. You will see VAT added onto the selling price on invoices, credit notes and some receipts. Shop till receipts generally do not show VAT.

Businesses with sales over a certain figure must by law register for VAT and are given a VAT registration number, which you see printed on invoices, often below the address.

In our Presto Supplies invoice on the previous page, copy paper and pencils costing £47.45 are charged VAT at 20%, which means that Wyvern Stationery have to pay VAT of £9.49, making an invoice total of £56.94.

DELIVERY NOTE

A **delivery note** is a document sent out with the order, giving details of the transaction. It is sometimes produced at the same time as the invoice.

Note that the delivery note shown below sets out a description of the goods, the product codes, quantities and Wyvern Stationery's purchase order number. These should tally with the details on the purchase order issued by the buyer. A delivery note does not have to show the price of the goods.

Delivery notes are dealt with in more detail in the next chapter.

DELIVERY NOTE

Presto Supplies
18 Fencote Road, Worcester WR2 6HY
Tel 01905 334482 email info@prestosupplies.com
VAT Reg 987 5441 21

Wyvern Stationery	number	12332
141, Bell Lane	delivery method	Parcelswift
Wyvern	purchase order	10450
WY1 4DB	date	12 12 2011

Product code	Quantity	Description
CP5R	2	A4 Alba copy paper (2500 pack)
PHB50	1	HB Pencils (50 pack)

DOCUMENTS FOR RETURNED GOODS

In the normal course of trading, and assuming the goods arrive safely, the invoice from Presto Supplies to Wyvern Stationery will be paid within 30 days of the invoice date, ie on or before 11 January 2012.

But what happens if there is a problem with the goods? Suppose one of the packs of copy paper has been crushed in transit and the package is so badly damaged that the paper is unusable.

The normal course of action here would be for the buyer, Wyvern Stationery, to note the defect on the **delivery note** (see previous page) and return the goods to Presto Supplies with a **goods returned note**. This is shown below.

GOODS RETURNED NOTE			**Wyvern Stationery**
			141, Bell Lane, Wyvern **WY1 4DB** Tel 01907 761234 Fax 01907 761987 Email info@wyvernstationery.co.uk VAT REG GB 0745 8383 56

supplier				
Presto Supplies 18 Fencote Road Worcester WR2 6HY			purchase order no	10450
			date	14 December 2011

Product code	Quantity	Description	Reason for return
CP5R	1	A4 Alba copy paper (2500 pack)	Goods damaged in transit

Note the details on this form which will enable Presto Supplies to tally up the returned goods with the sales order that they processed:

- the original purchase order number: 10450
- the product code of the goods supplied: CP5R
- the description of the goods

The next step will be for Presto Supplies to issue and send a **credit note** to Wyvern Stationery. This document will reduce the amount owed to Presto Supplies due for payment on or before 11 January 2012.

The credit note is illustrated and explained on the next two pages.

CREDIT NOTE

A **credit note** is a 'refund' document. It reduces the amount owed by the buyer. The goods, remember, have not yet been paid for.

The credit note is prepared by the seller and sent to the buyer. Situations where this might happen include:

- the goods may be damaged or faulty
- the goods may have been lost in transit
- incorrect goods may have been sent
- not enough goods have been sent

In the example transaction in this chapter, the staff of Wyvern Stationery have sent back to Presto Supplies a damaged pack of copy paper with a **goods returned note** which explains the problem. It will then be up to Presto Supplies to issue a **credit note** and send it to Wyvern Stationery. As Wyvern Stationery have not yet sent payment for the goods, the credit note reduces the amount they have to pay. Note that:

- the reason for the issue of the credit note is stated at the bottom of the document – here the reason is 'Goods damaged in transit'
- the format of the credit note is basically the same as an invoice

Now study the credit note on the opposite page and the explanatory notes below. The details filled in by Presto Supplies have a grey background.

the business giving the credit (refund)

the business receiving the credit (refund)

the credit note number, purchase order number and date

details of the item returned (note that these columns are the same as the columns on the invoice)

the reason for the return of the goods

the amount refunded includes the VAT, as on the invoice

the amount which will be deducted from the amount owed by the buyer of the goods

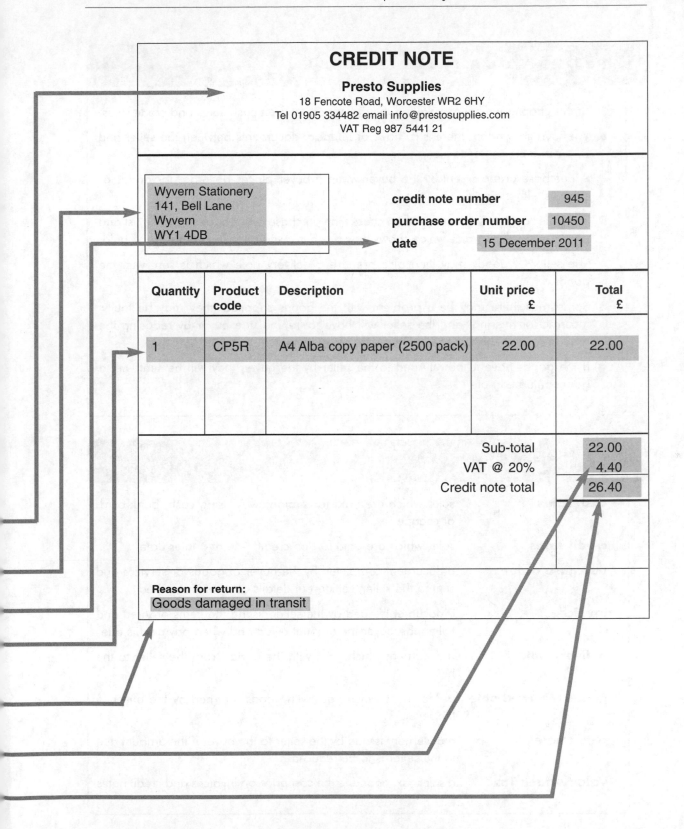

CREDIT NOTE

Presto Supplies
18 Fencote Road, Worcester WR2 6HY
Tel 01905 334482 email info@prestosupplies.com
VAT Reg 987 5441 21

Wyvern Stationery
141, Bell Lane
Wyvern
WY1 4DB

credit note number	945
purchase order number	10450
date	15 December 2011

Quantity	Product code	Description	Unit price £	Total £
1	CP5R	A4 Alba copy paper (2500 pack)	22.00	22.00
		Sub-total		22.00
		VAT @ 20%		4.40
		Credit note total		26.40

Reason for return:
Goods damaged in transit

Chapter summary

- In this chapter we have explained the difference between cash sales and credit sales.

- We have shown that there is a 'flow' of financial documents between the seller and buyer in a credit transaction.

- A purchase order is sent by the buyer when a buyer places an order for goods or services with the seller.

- The seller of goods or services then checks the purchase order against a price list and prepares a sales invoice which shows how much is owed and when it has to be paid.

- The seller of goods may then also prepare a delivery note which is sent with the goods.

- Sometimes there may be a problem with the goods supplied (they may be faulty, incorrect or missing) and the seller will have to 'refund' the buyer by reducing the amount owed. This is done by means of a credit note.

- If the goods have to be returned to the seller by the buyer, they will be sent with a goods returned note.

Key terms

cash sales	sales which are paid for straightaway using cash, bank card, or cheque
credit sales	sales which are paid for 'on credit' – ie at a later date
purchase order	a document completed by the buyer of goods or services and sent to the seller, setting out details of what is required
invoice	a document issued by the seller, listing the items ordered and telling the buyer the amount owed and when payment is due
delivery note	a document which goes with the goods from the seller to the buyer
goods returned note	a document which goes with goods returned by the buyer to the seller
credit note	a document issued by the seller to the buyer if the amount due to the seller is to be reduced
Value Added Tax	a sales tax, added to the cost price on invoices and credit notes

Exercises

Blank invoices and credit notes for use in these exercises are available at the back of this book, and also as downloads from the Resources section of www.osbornebooks.co.uk

Answers to the asterisked questions are to be found at the back of this book.

1.1* The definition of a cash sale is a sale made . . .

A   only with notes and coins

B   when payment is immediate

C   when payment can be made at a later date

Choose the correct option.

1.2 The definition of a credit sale is a sale made . . .

A   with a credit card

B   when payment is immediate

C   when payment is made at a later date

Choose the correct option.

1.3* A purchase order is a document . . .

A   issued by the seller and sent with the goods

B   issued by the buyer and setting out details of the goods

C   issued by the seller and setting out details of the goods

Choose the correct option.

1.4 A credit note is a document . . .

A   issued by the seller setting out the terms of a credit sale

B   issued by the buyer and sent with faulty goods being returned

C   issued by the seller when faulty goods have been returned

Choose the correct option.

1.5* If the total cost of goods on an invoice (after any discount) is £189.00 and Value Added Tax is 20%, the total amount payable by the customer is:

A   £226.80

B   £151.20

C   £37.80

Choose the correct option.

1.8　You have received the purchase order shown below. Using the details from this document and the price list provided, complete a sales invoice dated 15 December, ensuring that the document is completed with the correct product codes. The invoice number is the next number following on from the invoice prepared in the previous question. The VAT rate is 20%.

PURCHASE ORDER			**Wyvern Stationery**
			141, Bell Lane, Wyvern
			WY1 4DB
			Tel 01907 761234 Fax 01907 761987
			Email info@wyvernstationery.co.uk
			VAT REG GB 0745 8383 56

supplier			
Presto Supplies		**purchase order no**	10463
18 Fencote Road		**date**	13 December 2011
Worcester			
WR2 6HY			

product code	quantity	description
BFG	2	Senator foolscap box file, green @ £2.95
SFA4G	8	A4 suspension files, green (50 pack) @ £15.00
RBRD5	20	AlbaGel Rollerball, red (5 pack) @ £4.95

1.9*　You have received the goods returned note shown below. Using the details from this document and the price list provided, complete a sales credit note dated 15 December, ensuring that the document is completed with the correct product code. The sales credit note number is 946. The VAT rate to be used is 20%.

GOODS RETURNED NOTE			**Alpha Stationery**
			34 High Street
			Southbury SY1 4DB
			Tel 01906 451234
			Email sales@alphastationery.co.uk
			VAT REG GB 0645 2283 56

supplier			
Presto Supplies		**purchase order no**	1060
18 Fencote Road		**date**	12 December 2011
Worcester			
WR2 6HY			

Product code	Quantity	Description	Reason for return
PHB50	2	HB Pencils (50 pack)	Goods missing from consignment

1.10* You have received the goods returned note shown below. Using the details from this document and the price list provided, complete a sales credit note dated 15 December, ensuring that the document is completed with the correct product codes. The sales credit note number follows on from the sales credit note in the previous question. The VAT rate to be used is 20%.

GOODS RETURNED NOTE

Delphic Limited

34 Oracle Street
Walvern WA1 7ST
Tel 01706 654281 Email info@delphiclimited.co.uk
VAT REG GB 2645 3383 26

supplier
Presto Supplies
18 Fencote Road
Worcester
WR2 6HY

purchase order no   1945
date   12 December 2011

Product code	Quantity	Description	Reason for return
C4WSS	10	C4 Self-seal envelopes, white (250 pack)	Goods damaged in transit
SNY12	5	Sticky Notes, 76x76mm, yellow (12 Pack)	Goods damaged in transit

---

1.11 You have received the goods returned note shown below. Using the details from this document and the price list provided, complete a sales credit note dated 16 December, ensuring that the document is completed with the correct product code. The sales credit note number is 950. The VAT rate to be used is 20%.

GOODS RETURNED NOTE

Wyvern Stationery

141, Bell Lane, Wyvern
WY1 4DB
Tel 01907 761234 Fax 01907 761987
Email info@wyvernstationery.co.uk
VAT REG GB 0745 8383 56

supplier
Presto Supplies
18 Fencote Road
Worcester
WR2 6HY

purchase order no   10420
date   12 December 2011

Product code	Quantity	Description	Reason for return
RBBK5	5	AlbaGel Rollerball, black (5 pack)	Goods missing from consignment

2 Processing supplier invoices and credit notes

what this chapter covers . . .

This chapter:

- explains the need for the buyer to check invoices and credit notes received from suppliers for goods or services ordered, or goods returned

- describes the documents involved in this checking process; these include:
  - the purchase order – issued by the buyer ordering goods and services and setting out all the details of the order in the first place
  - the delivery note – issued and sent by the supplier – which sets out the details of the items being supplied
  - the supplier (purchase) invoice – issued by the supplier, setting out the details of the price charged, discounts given, Value Added Tax, and the total amount due
  - the supplier (purchase) credit note – issued by the supplier, normally when goods have been returned
  - the goods returned note – issued by the buyer and sent with the goods being returned – the details of which will have to be checked against the supplier's credit note to make sure the amount refunded is correct

- describes how errors and discrepancies in the documentation can be identified and what to do if a discrepancy is discovered

OCR assessment criteria covered

Unit M1: Preparing and processing bookkeeping documents

2.1 Check the accuracy of supplier invoices and credit notes against purchase orders, goods received and delivery notes

2.2 Check that agreed trade and bulk discounts have been applied accurately

2.3 Code supplier invoices and credit notes

PURCHASE DOCUMENTS

In the last chapter we described the processes carried out when, as the **seller** of goods and services, you issue:

- **sales invoices** – to obtain payment from the buyer for what you have sold on credit

- **sales credit notes** – to reduce the amount owed by the buyer, if, for example, goods have been returned

In this chapter we deal with the **same documents**, but from the point of view of the **buyer** of goods and services, who will need to check them carefully:

- **supplier invoices** – received from the supplier and payable by you

- **supplier credit notes** – to reduce the amount owed by you, if, for example, you return goods

If you look at the diagram below – it is basically the same diagram as shown in the last chapter – you will see that the documents involved are the same.

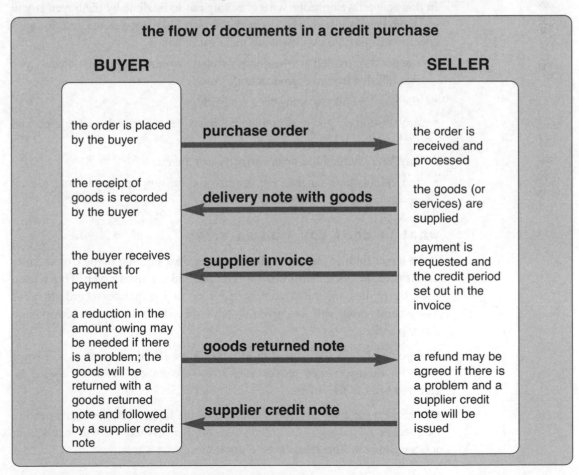

the flow of documents in a credit purchase

BUYER		SELLER
the order is placed by the buyer	**purchase order** →	the order is received and processed
the receipt of goods is recorded by the buyer	← **delivery note with goods**	the goods (or services) are supplied
the buyer receives a request for payment	← **supplier invoice**	payment is requested and the credit period set out in the invoice
a reduction in the amount owing may be needed if there is a problem; the goods will be returned with a goods returned note and followed by a supplier credit note	**goods returned note** → ← **supplier credit note**	a refund may be agreed if there is a problem and a supplier credit note will be issued

CHECKING THE DOCUMENTS

checking by the seller

In the last chapter it was seen as being very important to check for accuracy the main **sales documents** issued – the invoice and credit note. For example, checking:

- that the product codes of the goods invoiced are correct
- that the price charged is correct
- the calculations on the invoice, including the Value Added Tax, are all correct

If you make a mistake it could prove costly. Your level of customer service would look rather poor and payment could be delayed.

checking by the buyer

In this chapter we describe what checking has to be done by the buyer. If you are the buyer, you will need to check the **purchase documents**, and for very specific reasons: you will want to make sure that:

- the goods provided are the goods you have ordered in the first place – you can tell this from the product codes used
- the correct unit price has been charged
- any discounts you are entitled to have been correctly calculated and deducted
- any VAT charged has been correctly calculated
- the calculations on the supplier invoice or supplier credit note are all accurate

what to do if you find an error

If the buyer finds any errors or discrepancies on a supplier invoice or supplier credit note the document **must be rejected** and a reason given. This reason may be written on the document itself or in a separate record. In your assessments you will be given a table in which to record errors and discrepancies.

The golden rule is that **you should never alter the document** – an invoice total, for example – and process it as if it were correct. It should always be referred back to the seller.

On the next page we will explain in outline the main documents that need to be checked by the buyer who receives a supplier invoice. We will then set out a Case Study to illustrate all these principles.

what needs to be checked?

There are three documents involved in the checking process:

*   **purchase order**

    This is the first document to be issued. It is drawn up by the buyer to order the goods and will set out all the details of the purchase:
    – quantity
    – product code
    – description
    – unit price

*   **delivery note**

    This document is normally sent with the goods and is likely to be the first document relating to the transaction received by the buyer from the seller. The details on this document should be checked with the purchase order. The main question the buyer is asking here is "Has the supplier sent what we ordered?"

*   **supplier (purchase) invoice**

    This sets out what is owed by the buyer and when it has to be paid. This should be checked against the purchase order and delivery note. The questions the buyer is asking here are: "Are we being charged for what we ordered?" and "Are we being charged the right amount?"

This process is summarised on the diagram below and also explained in full in the Case Study which follows over the next few pages.

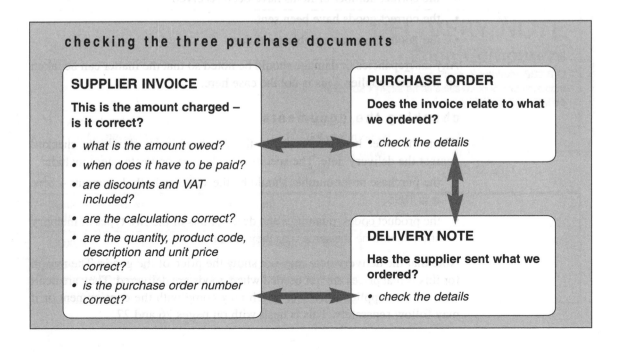

checking the three purchase documents

SUPPLIER INVOICE

This is the amount charged – is it correct?

*   what is the amount owed?
*   when does it have to be paid?
*   are discounts and VAT included?
*   are the calculations correct?
*   are the quantity, product code, description and unit price correct?
*   is the purchase order number correct?

PURCHASE ORDER

Does the invoice relate to what we ordered?

*   check the details

DELIVERY NOTE

Has the supplier sent what we ordered?

*   check the details

checking the supplier's (purchase) invoice

The invoice for the memory sticks is received by Aztex Limited from Zilon Computers the following day. It is shown on the next page. The invoice is checked against the delivery note and the purchase order. The specific points to look at (shown with a grey background) are:

- **invoice and delivery note**

  Are the details of the goods on the invoice and delivery note the same? The product code, description and quantity of the goods should agree.

- **invoice and purchase order**

  Has the invoice quoted the correct purchase order number? Has the correct price been charged? The unit price quoted by the supplier or obtained from the supplier's catalogue will be stated on the purchase order, and should agree with the unit price stated on the invoice. If there is a difference, it should be queried with the supplier.

checking the calculations on the invoice

All the calculations on the invoice should be checked; they are shown on the next page within dotted lines. If any of these calculations is incorrect, the final total will be wrong, and the invoice will have to be queried with the supplier. The checks to be made are:

- **quantity x unit price**

  The quantity of the items multiplied by the unit price must be correct. The result is used for the calculation of any discounts applicable.

- **trade discount**

  Trade discount is a percentage deduction from the normal list price; it is normally given to approved 'trade' customers. This discount is deducted from the total price. In the case of the invoice shown opposite, the total price worked out is £390. The 25% trade discount is shown and deducted on the line below the £390. The calculation is:

  $$£390 \ \times \ \frac{25}{100} \ = \ £97.50$$

  The price charged (on which VAT will be charged) is therefore:

  $$£390.00 \ - \ £97.50 \ = \ £292.50$$

- **bulk discount**

  Bulk discount is given for bulk purchases – ie large quantity purchases. If, for example, Aztex was to order 500 8GB memory sticks rather than just 10 it may be able to negotiate a further bulk discount.

  Bulk discount is calculated on the invoice in the same way as trade discount, ie it is deducted from the total price before the VAT is calculated and added on.

- **Value Added Tax (VAT)**

  Value Added Tax is a tax on sales. In this book VAT is calculated at 20%. On an invoice VAT is added to the total after the deduction of discount. The calculation on the invoice below is:

  $$£292.50 \times \frac{20}{100} = £58.50 = \text{VAT amount}$$

  If you are using a calculator, all you need to do is to multiply the total by 0.2 to give the VAT, which is then added to the total.

  Note that fractions of a penny are normally ignored when calculating VAT. If the VAT comes out on the calculator as £56.666666, the actual VAT should be £56.66 and is not rounded up to £56.67.

  Now study the invoice shown below and check the arithmetic.

KEY

arithmetic to check

check with purchase order and delivery note

INVOICE
Zilon Computers
8 Circus Place, Southbury, SB2 8VJ
Tel 01402 776152 email sales@ziloncomputers.com
VAT Reg 298 1662 85

Aztex Limited 29, Commercial Road Witton WT1 2HJ		

invoice number	2741
purchase order number	1095
date	12 December 2011

Quantity	Product code	Description	Unit price £	Total £
10	UDX08	8GB Ulex Memory Stick	15.00	150.00
8	UDX16	16GB Ulex Memory Stick	30.00	240.00
				390.00
		Less trade discount @ 25%		97.50
				292.50
		VAT @ 20%		58.50
		Invoice total		351.00

terms:
Net 30 days

DEALING WITH ERRORS AND DISCREPANCIES

what can go wrong?

There are are number of situations where a buyer checking the purchase documents and the delivered goods will find errors and discrepancies. In each case action will have to be taken by the buyer.

Some common examples of errors and discrepancies are listed below, together with examples of the action that will need to be taken in each case. You will find in commercial practice that the actions taken may vary to some extent, but the examples given below are fairly common. As you will see from the table there are two main situations:

- an **invoice with an error** on it should be rejected and a new invoice issued by the seller

- a **problem involving the goods** themselves – in these cases the goods should be returned to the supplier with a goods returned note and a credit note requested from the supplier

error/discrepancy	action to be taken
error in calculation on invoice	invoice rejected and not processed for payment
incorrect discount given on invoice	invoice rejected and not processed for payment
incorrect application of VAT on invoice	invoice rejected and not processed for payment
quantity of goods sent is too low	balance of goods sent <u>or</u> credit note requested
wrong goods sent	goods returned and credit note requested
faulty goods sent	goods returned and credit note requested
goods damaged in transit	goods returned and credit note requested

At the top of the next page is a **goods returned note** issued by Aztex to Zilon Computers and sent back with a faulty pocket hard drive supplied by Zilon. The **credit note** issued by Zilon Computers is at the bottom of the page. The following checks will need to be carried out on these documents:

- is the purchase order number the same?

- are the product code, quantity, description and unit price the same?

- has the trade discount (25%) been calculated and deducted correctly?

- has the VAT (20%) been calculated and added on correctly?

If there is an error or discrepancy on the credit note it will need to be recorded and the credit note will not be able to be passed on for processing. It would appear that the two documents shown here are in order.

GOODS RETURNED NOTE

Aztex Limited
29, Commercial Road
Witton WT1 2HJ
Tel 01723 654298 Fax 01723 654322 Email sales@aztex.co.uk
VAT REG GB 0347 7383 01

supplier
Zilon Computers
8 Circus Place
Southbury
SB2 8VJ

purchase order no 977
date 14 November 2011

Product code	Quantity	Description	Reason for return
HD109	1	Lazio 500GB pocket hard drive @ £80. 25% Trade discount.	Faulty goods

KEY

arithmetic to check

check with goods returned note and credit note

CREDIT NOTE
Zilon Computers
8 Circus Place, Southbury, SB2 8VJ
Tel 01402 776152 email sales@ziloncomputers.com
VAT Reg 298 1662 85

Aztex Limited
29, Commercial Road
Witton
WT1 2HJ

credit note number 151
purchase order number 977
date 21 November 2011

Quantity	Product code	Description	Unit price £	Total £
1	HD109	Lazio 500GB pocket hard drive	80.00	80.00
				80.00
		Less trade discount @ 25%		20.00
				60.00
		VAT @ 20%		12.00
		Credit note total		72.00

reason for credit:
Faulty goods

AN EXAMPLE OF ERRORS AND DISCREPANCIES

The documents on the previous page are both in order and therefore the credit note can be processed through the books of Aztex Limited. The result of this returns transaction will be that the amount owed by Aztex to Zilon Computers, its supplier, will be reduced by £72, ie the total of the credit note issued by Zilon Computers.

Your assessment is likely to require you to identify errors and discrepancies on these documents and to record them in a table. As an initial exercise, you should check the goods returned note below against the credit note on the next page. You will find a number of basic errors. Write them down, using the table at the bottom of this page if you wish, and compare your findings with the upside-down answer on the bottom of the next page. Hopefully errors on this scale will not be too common in the workplace!

GOODS RETURNED NOTE

Aztex Limited
29, Commercial Road
Witton WT1 2HJ
Tel 01723 654298 Fax 01723 654322 Email sales@aztex.co.uk
VAT REG GB 0347 7383 01

supplier
Zilon Computers
8 Circus Place
Southbury
SB2 8VJ

purchase order no   963
date   7 November 2011

Product code	Quantity	Description	Reason for return
WLK2W	1	Wireless keyboard (white) @ £60. 25% Trade discount.	Goods damaged in transit

Supplier	Purchase order number	Credit note number	Reason why credit note cannot be processed

CREDIT NOTE
Zilon Computers
8 Circus Place, Southbury, SB2 8VJ
Tel 01402 776152 email sales@ziloncomputers.com
VAT Reg 298 1662 85

Aztex Limited 29, Commercial Road Witton WT1 2HJ		

credit note number	2732
purchase order number	936
date	11 November 2011

Quantity	Product code	Description	Unit price £	Total £
1	WLK2W	Wireless keyboard (white)	60.00	60.00
				60.00
		Less trade discount @ 25%		12.00
				48.00
		VAT @ 20%		9.60
		Credit note total		38.40

reason for credit:
Goods damaged in transit

Supplier	Purchase order number	Credit note number	Reason why credit note cannot be processed
Zilon Computers	963	2732	Wrong purchase order number quoted Trade discount incorrectly calculated at 20% VAT should be added, not deducted

Chapter summary

- It is necessary for the buyer to check financial documentation relating to purchases in order to ensure that the goods received are:
  - the correct goods (ie the right quantity and the right specification)
  - charged at the correct price (including any discounts and Value Added Tax)

- When goods arrive from the supplier they should be checked against the delivery note sent with the goods.

- A purchase invoice should be checked against the purchase order issued by the buyer and the delivery note sent with the goods. If there are any errors or discrepancies, they should be noted and the purchase invoice should not be processed for payment.

- If goods are returned to the supplier, they should be sent back with a goods returned note. A purchases credit note will then be issued by the supplier.

- The purchases credit note should be checked against the goods returned note issued by the buyer. Any errors or discrepancies should be noted.

- When checking documents, particular attention should be paid to arithmetic accuracy, the level of discounts and treatment of Value Added Tax.

Key terms

supplier invoice	an invoice issued to the buyer by the supplier, setting out what is owed by the buyer and when it has to be paid
supplier credit note	a credit note issued to the buyer by the supplier, setting out a reduction in the amount owed to the supplier
purchase order	a document completed by the buyer of goods or services and sent to the seller, setting out details of what is required
delivery note	a document which goes with the goods from the seller to the buyer
goods returned note	a document which goes with goods returned by the the buyer to the seller
trade discount	a percentage reduction in the selling price of goods or services, normally given to trade customers who buy regularly
bulk discount	a percentage reduction in the selling price of goods or services, given for large quantity ('bulk') purchases

2.1* The documents that need to be checked when processing a supplier invoice for payment include:

    A   the invoice, the purchase order and the goods returned note

    B   the invoice, the price list and the goods returned note

    C   the invoice, the purchase order and the delivery note

Choose the correct option.

2.2 The documents that need to be checked when processing a supplier credit note when calculating the payment due include:

    A   the credit note and the delivery note

    B   the credit note and the goods returned note

    C   the invoice and the goods returned note

Choose the correct option.

2.3* Which of the following options best describes the term 'bulk discount'?

    A   a discount given to a customer who buys large quantities of goods

    B   a discount given to a very large customer

    C   a discount which avoids the need to charge VAT on an invoice

2.4 VAT is a tax which is shown on an invoice and

    A   is calculated on the cost of goods before discount is added on

    B   is calculated on the cost of goods after discount has been deducted

    C   is deducted from the cost of goods after discount has been calculated

Choose the correct option.

2.5* If you find that a supplier has made a simple arithmetic mistake on an invoice total, you should:

    A   not process the invoice because it is incorrect

    B   change the total to avoid further problems

    C   pass the invoice for payment because the total is lower than it should be

Choose the correct option.

2.6* The question that follows is based on the computer shop business, Aztex Limited, featured in this chapter. You are employed by this business as a bookkeeper.

During the course of November 2011 you are required to process a number of supplier credit notes which relate to items ordered which you have had to return for various reasons.

Your job here is to check the five credit notes and goods returned notes set out on the next five pages. If you find any errors or discrepancies you are required to complete the table below, setting out your reasons for not processing the credit notes. These pairs of documents are labelled (a) to (e) for ease of reference.

The current Value Added Tax (VAT) rate is 20%.

Supplier	Purchase order number	Credit note number	Reason why credit note cannot be processed

(a)

GOODS RETURNED NOTE

Aztex Limited

29, Commercial Road
Witton WT1 2HJ

Tel 01723 654298 Fax 01723 654322 Email sales@aztex.co.uk
VAT REG GB 0347 7383 01

supplier

Zilon Computers
8 Circus Place
Southbury
SB2 8VJ

purchase order no   950

date   7 November 2011

Product code	Quantity	Description	Reason for return
HD110	2	Lazio 1TB pocket hard drive @ £120. 25% Trade discount.	Goods damaged in transit

CREDIT NOTE
Zilon Computers

8 Circus Place, Southbury, SB2 8VJ
Tel 01402 776152 email sales@ziloncomputers.com
VAT Reg 298 1662 85

Aztex Limited
29, Commercial Road
Witton
WT1 2HJ

credit note number   2703

purchase order number   950

date   10 November 2011

Quantity	Product code	Description	Unit price £	Total £
1	HD110	Lazio 1TB pocket hard drive	120.00	120.00
				120.00
		Less trade discount @ 20%		24.00
				96.00
		VAT @ 20%		19.20
		Credit note total		115.20

reason for credit:
Goods damaged in transit

(b)

GOODS RETURNED NOTE

Aztex Limited

29, Commercial Road
Witton WT1 2HJ

Tel 01723 654298 Fax 01723 654322 Email sales@aztex.co.uk
VAT REG GB 0347 7383 01

supplier
Droitwich Digital
19 Kidder Estate
Droitwich
DW3 8JG

purchase order no   955
date   8 November 2011

Product code	Quantity	Description	Reason for return
LMS16	10	Letho 16GB memory sticks @ £19.95. 20% Trade discount.	Goods damaged in transit

CREDIT NOTE

Droitwich Digital

19 Kidder Estate, Droitwich, DW3 8JG
Tel 01905 772191 email sales@droitwichdigital.co.uk
VAT Reg 244 1694 88

Aztex Limited
29, Commercial Road
Witton
WT1 2HJ

credit note number   1789

purchase order number   955

date   14 November 2011

Quantity	Product code	Description	Unit price £	Total £
10	LMS08	Letho 16GB memory sticks	8.00	80.00
				80.00
		Less trade discount @ 20%		16.00
				96.00
		VAT @ 20%		19.20
		Credit note total		115.20

reason for credit:
Goods damaged in transit

(c)

GOODS RETURNED NOTE

Aztex Limited
29, Commercial Road
Witton WT1 2HJ
Tel 01723 654298 Fax 01723 654322 Email sales@aztex.co.uk
VAT REG GB 0347 7383 01

supplier
Delphic Limited
34 Oracle Street
Walvern
WA1 7ST

purchase order no   977

date   9 November 2011

Product code	Quantity	Description	Reason for return
OM120	5	Topo optical mouse @ 18.00. Trade discount @ 15%.	Incorrect goods supplied.

CREDIT NOTE

Delphic Limited
34 Oracle Street
Walvern WA1 7ST
Tel 01706 654281 Email info@delphiclimited.co.uk
VAT Reg GB 2645 3383 26

Aztex Limited
29, Commercial Road
Witton
WT1 2HJ

credit note number   1924

purchase order number   977

date   16 November 2011

Quantity	Product code	Description	Unit price £	Total £
5	OM120	Topo optical mouse	18.00	90.00
				90.00
		Less trade discount @ 15%		13.50
				76.50
		VAT @ 20%		15.50
		Credit note total		92.00

reason for credit:
Incorrect goods supplied

(d)

GOODS RETURNED NOTE

Aztex Limited

29, Commercial Road
Witton WT1 2HJ
Tel 01723 654298 Fax 01723 654322 Email sales@aztex.co.uk
VAT REG GB 0347 7383 01

supplier
Presto Supplies
18 Fencote Road
Worcester
WR2 6HY

purchase order no	981
date	10 November 2011

Product code	Quantity	Description	Reason for return
SNC6	10	Sticky Notes (coloured) 6 pack @ 6.95. 20% Trade discount.	Duplicated order

CREDIT NOTE

Presto Supplies

18 Fencote Road, Worcester WR2 6HY
Tel 01905 334482 email info@prestosupplies.com
VAT Reg 987 5441 21

Aztex Limited
29, Commercial Road
Witton
WT1 2HJ

credit note number	907
purchase order number	981
date	17 November 2011

Quantity	Product code	Description	Unit price £	Total £
10	SNC6	Sticky notes (coloured) 6 pack	6.95	69.50
				69.50
		Less trade discount @ 20%		13.90
				55.60
		VAT @ 20%		11.12
		Credit note total		66.72

reason for credit:
Duplicated order

(e)

GOODS RETURNED NOTE

Aztex Limited
29, Commercial Road
Witton WT1 2HJ
Tel 01723 654298 Fax 01723 654322 Email sales@aztex.co.uk
VAT REG GB 0347 7383 01

supplier

Zilon Computers
8 Circus Place
Southbury
SB2 8VJ

purchase order no	982
date	15 November 2011

Product code	Quantity	Description	Reason for return
TB100	1	Troybuster anti-virus software @ £48.00. Trade discount 25%.	Wrong version of software sent

CREDIT NOTE
Zilon Computers
8 Circus Place, Southbury, SB2 8VJ
Tel 01402 776152 email sales@ziloncomputers.com
VAT Reg 298 1662 85

Aztex Limited
29, Commercial Road
Witton
WT1 2HJ

credit note number	2732
purchase order number	928
date	22 November 2011

Quantity	Product code	Description	Unit price £	Total £
1	TB100	Troybuster anti-virus software	40.00	40.00
				40.00
		Less trade discount @ 25%		8.00
				32.00
		VAT @ 20%		6.40
		Credit note total		38.40

reason for credit:
Wrong version of software sent

3 From documents to day books

This chapter:

● explains the need for the information contained on financial documents such as invoices and credit notes to be summarised; this information includes
  • the date
  • the name of the business issuing the document
  • the total cost of the goods
  • Value Added Tax
  • the final total of the document

● describes how this financial information is transferred from invoices to
  • the sales day book, which summarises the sales invoices
  • the purchase day book, which summarises the purchase invoices

● describes how this financial information is transferred from credit notes to
  • the sales returns day book, which summarises the sales credit notes
  • the purchase returns day book, which summarises the purchase credit notes

● describes how the day books are totalled and then the totals added up as a cross check for accuracy to ensure that the totals are correct

OCR assessment criteria covered

Unit M2: Recording credit transactions

1.1 Enter the information taken from invoices and credit notes into the following analysed day books:

  • Sales day book and Sales returns day book

  • Purchase day book and Purchase returns day book

1.2 Total and cross check the day books for accuracy

WRITING UP THE DAY BOOKS

what is a day book?

A day book is a summary list of financial transactions, compiled from financial documents such as invoices and credit notes.

A day book is the source of data needed for entering information into the accounts of a business. The accounts provide important information to the managers of a business about its income and expenses, its sales and purchases, for example.

You will not need to study the accounts at this qualification level, but it is useful to know why day books are so important in the accounting system.

The diagram below shows how a day book fits into the accounting system.

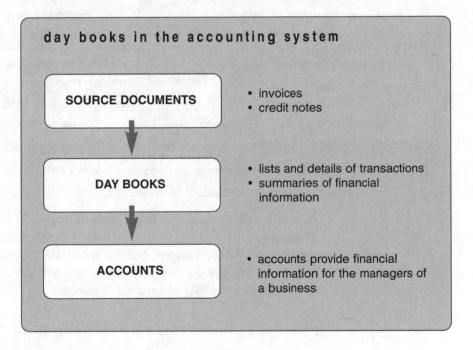

A day book therefore acts as the link between the invoices and credit notes shown in the last two chapters - the **source documents** - and the accounts which are needed to record all aspects of credit purchases and credit sales.

Until the various day books are completed, all the business will have to show for its credit sales and purchases and returns will be piles of invoices and credit notes. The day books organise and summarise all this information into a manageable form.

types of day book

There are a number of different day books, each dealing with a different type of transaction. In your assessment you will have to write entries in four day books:

- **purchase day book** - details from **purchase invoices** sent by suppliers

- **purchase returns day book** - details from **purchase credit notes** received from suppliers

- **sales day book** - details from **sales invoices** sent to customers

- **sales returns day book** - details from **sales credit notes** issued to customers

This is shown in the diagram below.

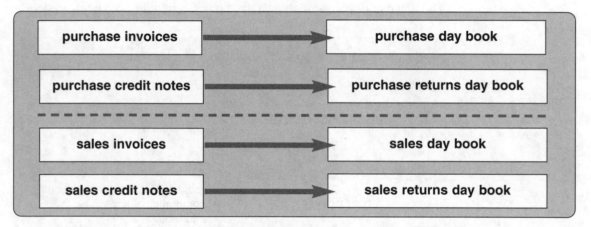

Before describing these day books we will firstly summarise the four types of document that you will be dealing with. You should have already covered these in the last two chapters, but it is important that you should be able to recognise each type because your assessment will not tell you – all you will be faced with is a series of unsorted documents.

purchase invoices and purchase credit notes

A **purchase invoice** is an invoice received by a business which has bought goods and services from a supplier. When you deal with a business scenario in an assessment you need to think about a purchase invoice as the document which is **received by you** from someone else.

In the same way, if you have **purchased** faulty goods you will be doing the returning and the faulty goods become **purchase returns**, because you are **returning** them and receiving a purchase credit note.

This is summarised in the diagram at the top of the next page.

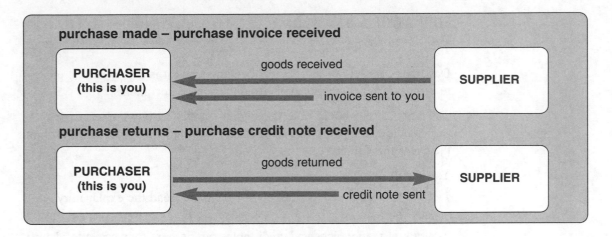

sales invoices and sales credit notes

A **sales invoice** is an invoice issued by a business which is selling goods and services. When you deal with a business scenario in the assessment, you need to think about a sales invoice as the document which is **issued by you**.

A **sales credit note** is issued in the case of **sales returns**. This is easy to understand because it means that if you are the **seller**, the goods are being **returned** to you and so a credit note will have to be issued by you.

This is summarised in the diagram below.

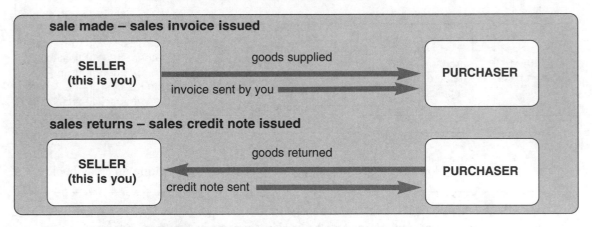

assessment tips

1 Identify the name of the seller (ie you).

2 Identify the documents issued by the seller by looking at the name at the top of the document – if you wish, write 'Sales Invoice' or 'Sales Credit Note' or 'SI' or 'SCN' next to the appropriate document.

3 Identify the remaining documents as Purchase Invoices and Purchase Credit Notes.

You should now be ready to write up the day books.

FORMAT OF A DAY BOOK

Day books are set out in a series of columns and it is a very simple process to enter up the necessary details from the source documents.

The purchase day book for a sports goods supply business – Zest Sports – is shown below, and purchase and sales invoices and credit notes are shown on the pages that follow.

You should:

1   Study the day book format on this page and read the explanatory notes that follow.

2   Look at the invoices and credit notes on the next four pages to identify the source of the information which is entered in each of the four day books. You can do this by following the arrows.

Purchase Day Book

Date	Details		Goods	VAT	Total
2011			£	£	£
11 Oct	AB Supplies		112.00	22.40	134.40

| The date is the date of the purchase invoice. | The details are the name of the supplier. | | The 'goods' column shows the cost of the goods after deduction of any trade or bulk discount. | VAT is charged and added to the cost of goods. | This is the final total owing to the supplier. |

Note also the following points to observe when writing up a day book:

Date	• the year date is shown on the first line • the month and day date of the invoice is entered on the lines underneath • you should never enter a ditto mark (") in the date column
Details	• this is the name of the supplier and <u>not</u> the goods
£ signs	• there is a £ sign on the first line of the three money columns
Goods	• this is the amount owing <u>before</u> VAT is added on but <u>after</u> deduction of trade or bulk discount

The layout of the Sales Day Book is exactly the same (see page 47).

purchase invoice to purchase day book

On this page you can see, by following the arrows, where the information for the **purchase day book** can be found on a purchase invoice.

INVOICE

AB Supplies Limited

Unit 16 Millyard Estate, Milton Keynes MK7 9GF
Tel 01908 321727 email info@absupplies.co.uk
VAT Reg 423 9663 77

Zest Sports
Unit 16 Fencote Road,
Worcester WR2 6HY

invoice number   87522

date   24 October 2011

Quantity	Description	Unit price £	Total £
10	Footballs 5141	8.00	80.00
5	Footballs 8761	12.00	60.00
			140.00
	Less 15% trade discount		21.00
			119.00
	VAT at 20%		23.80
	Invoice total		142.80

terms: 30 days

Purchase Day Book

Date	Details	Goods £	VAT £	Total £
2011				
24 Oct	AB Supplies	119.00	23.80	142.80

purchase credit note to purchase returns day book

On this page you can see, by following the arrows, where the information for the **purchase returns day book** can be found on a purchase credit note.

CREDIT NOTE

AB Supplies Limited

Unit 16 Millyard Estate, Milton Keynes MK7 9GF
Tel 01908 321727 email info@absupplies.co.uk
VAT Reg 423 9663 77

Zest Sports
Unit 16 Fencote Road,
Worcester WR2 6HY

credit note number   452

date   30 October 2011

Quantity	Description	Unit price £	Total £
2	Footballs 5141	8.00	16.00
			16.00
	Less 15% trade discount		2.40
			13.60
	VAT at 20%		2.72
	Invoice total		16.32

reason for credit: damaged goods

Purchase Returns Day Book

Date	Details	Goods	VAT	Total
2011		£	£	£
30 Oct	AB Supplies	13.60	2.72	16.32

sales invoice to sales day book

On this page you can see, by following the arrows, where the information for the **sales day book** can be found on a sales invoice.

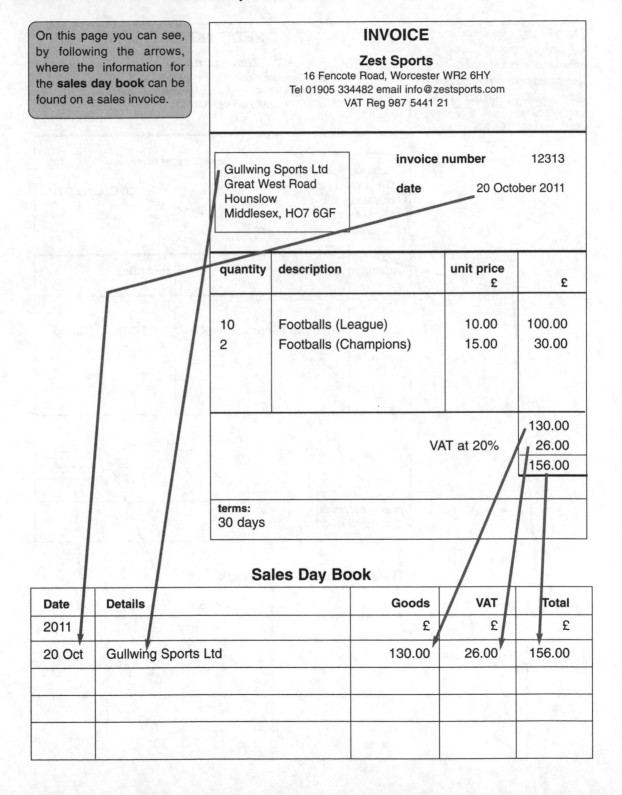

INVOICE

Zest Sports
16 Fencote Road, Worcester WR2 6HY
Tel 01905 334482 email info@zestsports.com
VAT Reg 987 5441 21

Gullwing Sports Ltd
Great West Road
Hounslow
Middlesex, HO7 6GF

| invoice number | 12313 |
| date | 20 October 2011 |

quantity	description	unit price £	£
10	Footballs (League)	10.00	100.00
2	Footballs (Champions)	15.00	30.00
			130.00
	VAT at 20%		26.00
			156.00

terms:
30 days

Sales Day Book

Date	Details	Goods	VAT	Total
2011		£	£	£
20 Oct	Gullwing Sports Ltd	130.00	26.00	156.00

sales credit note to sales returns day book

On this page you can see, by following the arrows, where the information for the **sales returns day book** can be found on a sales credit note.

CREDIT NOTE

Zest Sports
16 Fencote Road, Worcester WR2 6HY
Tel 01905 334482 email info@zestsports.com
VAT Reg 987 5441 21

Gullwing Sports Ltd
Great West Road
Hounslow
Middlesex, HO7 6GF

credit note number   715

date   26 October 2011

quantity	description	unit price £	£
2	Footballs (Champions)	15.00	30.00
			30.00
	VAT at 20%		6.00
			36.00

reason for credit:
damaged goods

Sales Returns Day Book

Date	Details	Goods	VAT	Total
2011		£	£	£
26 Oct	Gullwing Sports Ltd	30.00	6.00	36.00

TOTALLING THE DAY BOOKS – CROSS CASTING

When the day books have been written up over a period of time, a month for example, the next step is to **total up** the various money columns in the day book on a single 'totals' line at the end of that period. It is important to remember to enter the date at the beginning of the last line – this is normally the last day of the month.

The totals should then be carefully checked by **cross casting**. This means adding up all the money totals from left to right – except the 'Total' column – and checking that this calculated figure agrees with the total of the 'Total' column. If it does not there must be an error in the figures which will have to be traced and corrected.

The totalled purchase day book for Zest Sports for the month of August 2011 is shown below. Study the figures on the bottom line and read the notes in the boxes underneath.

Purchase Day Book

Date	Details	Goods	VAT	Total
2011		£	£	£
5 Aug	AB Supplies	80.00	16.00	96.00
12 Aug	S Gerrard Limited	120.00	24.00	144.00
15 Aug	Murray Enterprises	200.00	40.00	240.00
24 Aug	Hermes Sports	60.00	12.00	72.00
30 Aug	AB Supplies	96.00	19.20	115.20
31 Aug		556.00	111.20	667.20

Step 1
Write in the date on which you are totalling the day book – normally it is the last day of the month

Step 2
Total the Goods column

Step 3
Total the VAT column

Step 4
Total the Total column

Step 5 – 'cross cast'
Add up the two totals obtained in Steps 2 and 3. Compare this total with the 'Total' total (Step 4). If it agrees, the day book is correct. If it does not agree, there is an error in the figures which will have to be identified and corrected.

Chapter summary

- A daybook is a summary of financial transactions which forms a link between source documents (invoices and credit notes) and the accounting records of a business.

- There are four day books:
  - purchase day book, which lists purchase invoices
  - purchase returns daybook, which lists purchase credit notes
  - sales day book, which lists sales invoices
  - sales returns daybook, which lists sales credit notes

- The details recorded in columns in a day book include:
  - the date of the invoice or credit note
  - the name of the business issuing the document
  - the total cost of the goods
  - Value Added Tax
  - the final total of the document

- The money amount columns in a day book are totalled periodically and the Goods and VAT totals added up to check that they agree ('cross cast') with the final total column. Any discrepancies should be investigated.

Key terms

day book	a list and summary of financial transactions compiled from source documents such as invoices and credit notes
purchase day book	a daybook which lists details on purchase invoices
purchase returns daybook	a daybook which lists details on purchase credit notes
sales day book	a daybook which lists details on sales invoices
sales returns daybook	a daybook which lists details on sales credit notes
cross casting	adding up the money columns (the Goods and VAT columns on day book) and checking that the totals of these columns equals the total of the final total column

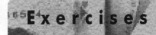

3.1* A number of invoices and credit notes were issued and received by Campbell Designs during October 2011. Campbell Designs is an art materials wholesaler. The accounts assistant has already sorted the documents into date order and also by day book.

The date is 31 October 2011.

You are to enter up these transactions in the appropriate day books, total the money columns and cross cast the totals to check your accuracy. Remember to write the headings in the day books.

purchase invoices

date	supplier name	goods supplied	VAT	Invoice total
24 Oct	J Miller Ltd	£80.00	£16.00	£96.00
25 Oct	Hirst Supplies	£168.00	£33.60	£201.60
27 Oct	Turner & Co	£48.00	£9.60	£57.60
28 Oct	Manet Ltd	£96.00	£19.20	£115.20

purchase returns credit notes

date	supplier name	goods supplied	VAT	Credit Note total
26 Oct	J Macmillan	£16.00	£3.20	£19.20
28 Oct	J Constable	£64.00	£12.80	£76.80

sales invoices

date	customer name	goods supplied	VAT	Invoice total
24 Oct	Coppola Ltd	£304.00	£60.80	£364.80
26 Oct	J Mason	£88.00	£17.60	£105.60
27 Oct	Cute Shop	£120.00	£24.00	£144.00
28 Oct	P Casso	£152.00	£30.40	£182.40

sales returns credit notes

date	customer name	goods supplied	VAT	Credit Note total
25 Oct	Coppola Ltd	£56.00	£11.20	£67.20
27 Oct	J Steinbeck	£72.00	£14.40	£86.40

3.2   A batch of invoices and credit notes was issued and received by Campbell Designs during the last two weeks of November 2011.

The accounts assistant has already sorted the documents into date order and also by day book.

The date is 30 November 2011.

Your job is to enter up these transactions in the appropriate day books, total the money columns and cross cast the totals to check your accuracy. Remember to write the headings in the day books.

purchase invoices

date	supplier name	goods supplied	VAT	Invoice total
21 Nov	T M Inn Ltd	£120.00	£24.00	£144.00
23 Nov	Hirst Supplies	£144.00	£28.80	£172.80
25 Nov	T M Inn Ltd	£32.00	£6.40	£38.40
28 Nov	Hirst Supplies	£184.00	£36.80	£220.80

purchase returns credit notes

date	supplier name	goods supplied	VAT	Credit Note total
25 Nov	J Miller	£16.00	£3.20	£19.20
29 Nov	Manet Ltd	£10.00	£2.00	£12.00

sales invoices

date	customer name	goods supplied	VAT	Invoice total
22 Nov	R Khan	£72.00	£14.40	£86.40
24 Nov	Wong Art	£128.00	£25.60	£153.60
25 Nov	Carmen Corner	£220.00	£44.00	£264.00
28 Nov	R M Brandt	£356.00	£71.20	£427.20

sales returns credit notes

date	customer name	goods supplied	VAT	Credit Note total
24 Nov	P Casso	£32.00	£6.40	£38.40
28 Nov	Cute Shop	£56.00	£11.20	£67.20

3.3* This exercise continues the Case Study of Zest Sports, a specialist sports goods supplier.

The date is 30 November 2011. The accounts assistant has been handed the purchase and sales invoices and credit notes for the last two weeks of the month. They have been sorted into four piles:

- purchase invoices
- purchase returns credit notes
- sales invoices

sales returns credit notes

ob is to write these transactions in the appropriate day books in date order, total the money and cross cast the totals to check your accuracy.

INVOICE

AB Supplies Limited

Unit 16 Millyard Estate, Milton Keynes MK7 9GF
Tel 01908 321727 email info@absupplies.co.uk
VAT Reg 423 9663 77

| Zest Sports
Unit 16 Fencote Road,
Worcester WR2 6HY | invoice number | 87571 |
| | date | 21 November 2011 |

quantity	description	unit price £	£	£
10	Footballs 5141	8.00	80.00	
10	Footballs 8761	12.00	120.00	
			200.00	
	Less 20% trade discount		40.00	
				160.00
	VAT at 20%			32.00
				192.00

terms:
30 days

INVOICE

N Mehta Limited

17, Market Street, Middleton MI5 6HP

Tel 01709 826421 email sales@nmehta.com

VAT Reg 723 3863 37

| Zest Sports
Unit 16 Fencote Road,
Worcester WR2 6HY | **invoice number** | | 7261 |
| | **date** | | 23 November 2011 |

quantity	description	unit price £	£	£
24	Footballs Ref FB88	9.00	216.00	
15	Footballs Ref FB95	12.50	187.50	
			403.50	
	Less 20% trade discount		80.70	
				322.80
	VAT at 20%			64.56
				387.36

terms:
30 days

INVOICE

AB Supplies Limited

Unit 16 Millyard Estate, Milton Keynes MK7 9GF
Tel 01908 321727 email info@absupplies.co.uk
VAT Reg 423 9663 77

| Zest Sports
Unit 16 Fencote Road,
Worcester WR2 6HY | invoice number | 87579 |
| | date | 28 November 2011 |

quantity	description	unit price £	£	£
16	Footballs 5141	8.00	128.00	
20	Footballs 8761	12.00	240.00	
			368.00	
	Less 20% trade discount		73.60	
				294.40
	VAT at 20%			58.88
				353.28

terms:
30 days

CREDIT NOTE

AB Supplies Limited

Unit 16 Millyard Estate, Milton Keynes MK7 9GF
Tel 01908 321727 email info@absupplies.co.uk
VAT Reg 423 9663 77

Zest Sports
Unit 16 Fencote Road,
Worcester WR2 6HY

credit note number   454

date   25 November 2011

quantity	description	unit price £	£	£
2	Footballs 8761	12.00	24.00	
	Less 20% trade discount		4.80	
				19.20
	VAT at 20%			3.84
				23.04

Reason for credit:
Cancelled order

CREDIT NOTE

N Mehta Limited

17, Market Street, Middleton MI5 6HP

Tel 01709 826421 email sales@nmehta.com

VAT Reg 723 3863 37

Zest Sports Unit 16 Fencote Road, Worcester WR2 6HY	**credit note number** 967 **date** 28 November 2009

quantity	description	unit price £	£	£
4	Footballs Ref FB88	9.00	36.00	
	Less 20% trade discount		7.20	
				28.80
	VAT at 20%			5.76
				34.56

reason for credit:
Faulty goods

INVOICE

Zest Sports

16 Fencote Road, Worcester WR2 6HY
Tel 01905 334482 email info@zestsports.com
VAT Reg 987 5441 21

| Gullwing Sports Ltd
Great West Road
Hounslow
Middlesex, HO7 6GF | **invoice number** | 12331 |
| | **date** | 22 November 2011 |

quantity	description	unit price £	£
20	Footballs (League)	10.00	200.00
8	Footballs (Champions)	15.00	120.00
			320.00
	VAT at 20%		64.00
			384.00

terms:
30 days

INVOICE

Zest Sports

16 Fencote Road, Worcester WR2 6HY
Tel 01905 334482 email info@zestsports.com
VAT Reg 987 5441 21

| Kerrison Sports
44, Kilmersdon Road
Bath
BA1 5FG | **invoice number** | 12332 |
| | **date** | 23 November 2011 |

quantity	description	unit price £	£
5	Practice Tennis Balls (box)	20.00	100.00
2	Centre Court Balls (box)	16.00	32.00
			132.00
	VAT at 20%		26.40
			158.40

terms:
30 days

INVOICE

Zest Sports

16 Fencote Road, Worcester WR2 6HY
Tel 01905 334482 email info@zestsports.com
VAT Reg 987 5441 21

Gullwing Sports Ltd
Great West Road
Hounslow
Middlesex, HO7 6GF

invoice number   12333

date   25 November 2011

quantity	description	unit price £	£
15	Footballs (League)	10.00	150.00
5	Footballs (Champions)	15.00	75.00
			225.00
	VAT at 20%		45.00
			270.00

terms:
30 days

INVOICE

Zest Sports

16 Fencote Road, Worcester WR2 6HY
Tel 01905 334482 email info@zestsports.com
VAT Reg 987 5441 21

Kerrison Sports 44, Kilmersdon Road Bath BA1 5FG	**invoice number** 12334 **date** 28 November 2011

quantity	description	unit price £	£
7	Practice Tennis Balls (box)	20.00	140.00
3	Centre Court Balls (box)	16.00	48.00
			188.00
	VAT at 20%		37.60
			225.60

terms:
30 days

CREDIT NOTE

Zest Sports

16 Fencote Road, Worcester WR2 6HY
Tel 01905 334482 email info@zestsports.co.uk
VAT Reg 987 5441 21

| Gullwing Sports Ltd
Great West Road
Hounslow
Middlesex, HO7 6GF | credit note number | 723 |
| | date | 28 November 2011 |

quantity	description	unit price £	£
4	Footballs (Champions)	15.00	60.00
			60.00
	VAT at 20%		12.00
			72.00

reason for credit:
shortage in delivery

CREDIT NOTE

Zest Sports
16 Fencote Road, Worcester WR2 6HY
Tel 01905 334482 email info@zestsports.co.uk
VAT Reg 987 5441 21

Kerrison Sports 44, Kilmersdon Road Bath BA1 5FG	**credit note number** 724 **date** 29 November 2011

quantity	description	unit price £	£
1	Practice Tennis Balls (box)	20.00	20.00
			20.00
	VAT at 20%		4.00
			24.00

reason for credit:
damaged goods

4 Receiving payments

what this chapter covers . . .

This chapter:

- describes the various ways in which businesses receive payments from their customers; these include cash, cheques, bank giro credits, Bankers Automated Clearing System (BACS) transfers and Clearing House Automated Payment System (CHAPS) payments

- explains the procedures for handling cash, including receipts from cash sales, accounting for the cash received, dealing with a cash float and banking the remaining cash using a paying-in slip

- describes how cheques are checked to make sure they are in order when they are received, and how they are paid into the bank on a paying-in slip

- describes the format of an Outstanding Invoice List and the way it is used to monitor the receipt of payments

- explains the format and use of a bank statement

- identifies from the bank statement payments received direct into the business bank account and describes how these receipts are recorded on the Outstanding Invoice List

OCR assessment criteria covered

Unit M3: Making and receiving payments

1.1 Check supporting documents against cash received

1.2 Prepare a till contents sheet or equivalent and reconcile daily takings

1.3 Prepare notes and coins for banking by completing a paying-in slip

2.1 Identify whether cheques received are valid

2.2 Check supporting documents against payments received

2.3 Prepare cheques for banking by completing a paying-in slip

INCOMING PAYMENTS

Payments can be received by a business in a variety of ways. The methods required for your studies are:

- cash (ie banknotes and coins)
- cheques
- payments direct to the bank by inter-bank transfer: Bankers Automated Clearing System (BACS) and Clearing House Automated Payment System (CHAPS)

We will now explain these in turn.

CASH

Cash is still one of the simplest methods of making payment for goods and services, particularly where small amounts are involved. There are, however, a number of risks involved in handling cash.

guidelines for cash handling

Cash is often a target for theft – and not only from people outside the business! General security guidelines for looking after cash received will vary according to the size of the business:

- cash should be kept in a secure place, for example in a cash till or cash box which should be kept locked and the keys retained under the control of the cashier
- as little cash as is practically possible should be kept in tills
- cash should be checked to ensure that it corresponds with any documentation showing the amount received
- the correct change must be given
- cash should be paid into the bank as soon as possible

receipts of payments in cash

For a business receiving sums of money in the form of cash it is necessary for the cashier to count the cash received and check it against the amount handed over. Change will need to be given when the exact amount is not paid. For example if someone buys a book costing £15.99 and hands over a £20 note:

Sale of book	£15.99
Amount given by customer	£20.00
Change to be given by shop	£ 4.01

The amount of change is the difference between the amount handed over and the amount of the sale. When payment is made in cash a receipt may be given, as shown below:

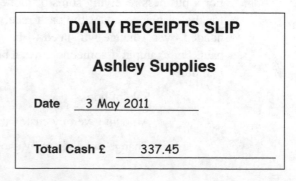

RECEIPT		
Ashley Supplies		
Date 3 May 2011		**No** 43
Received from L Mehta		
The sum of Ten pounds and sixty seven pence		
Cheque		
Cash	10	67
Signed S Ashley		
WITH THANKS		

Here the receipt for £10.67 is issued by Ashley Supplies to L Mehta.

Daily Receipts Slip

If the business issues a number of receipts for cash received during the day it can add up the receipt amounts and record the total on a **Daily Receipts Slip**, as shown on the example below. This shows that a total of £337.45 has been received during the day. This amount will need to be accounted for on a **Till Contents Sheet** (see next page).

DAILY RECEIPTS SLIP

Ashley Supplies

Date   3 May 2011

Total Cash £   337.45

'cashing up', cash floats and Till Contents Sheet

At the end of each day it is necessary to '**cash up**' by totalling the cash held and then agreeing that total with the amount in the till at the beginning of the day (the **cash float**) plus what has been received during the day (recorded on the **Daily Receipts Slip** shown on the previous page).

The amount in the till at the end of the day should therefore be:

cash float at start

plus sales made during the day (the Daily Receipts Slip)

equals amount of cash held at end of day

The cash float will need to be kept back for the following day, and the surplus will be entered on a paying-in slip for paying into the bank.

All this will be recorded on the **Till Contents Sheet**, shown below. Study the form and then read the guidance notes on the next page.

TILL CONTENTS SHEET					
Date 3 May 2011			**Float**		
Notes	**Quantity**	**Total**	**Notes**	**Quantity**	**Total**
£20	12	240.00	£20		
£10	7	70.00	£10	1	10.00
£5	7	35.00	£5	2	10.00
Coins			**Coins**		
£2	4	8.00	£2	2	4.00
£1	13	13.00	£1	10	10.00
50p	17	8.50	50p	10	5.00
20p	18	3.60	20p	10	2.00
10p	16	1.60	10p	15	1.50
5p	13	0.65	5p	12	0.60
2p	38	0.76	2p	30	0.60
1p	34	0.34	1p	30	0.30
Cash Total		381.45	**Float Total**		44.00
			CASH TO BANK		337.45

The float - the total of the cash in the till held over for the next day

The total of the cash in the till at the end of the day.

The surplus of cash to be paid into the bank = Cash Total minus Float Total = Daily Receipts Slip total

notes on the Till Contents Sheet

In your assessment you are likely to have to carry out a number of tasks relating to taking in cash and entering figures on the Till Contents Sheet. Tasks may include:

1　Adding up the amounts on a number of cash receipts to produce a total for the Daily Receipts Slip.

2　Completing the Cash Total in the Till Contents Sheet from given quantities of cash.

3　Completing the Float Total in the Till Contents Sheet from given quantities of cash.

4　Calculating the amount to be paid into the bank (ie Cash Total minus Float Total) and agreeing this with the Daily Receipts Slip total.

5　Using the figures in the 'Quantity' columns to work out what notes and coins you have available to pay in at the bank (after keeping the float on one side) – these will then be entered on a paying-in slip (see below). Note that the business may place the paying-in slip and cash in a secure wallet known as a 'night safe' which can be lodged with the bank overnight for safety.

The completed **paying-in slip** is shown below. Note that it is:

- dated
- completed with the details of the notes and coins being paid in
- totalled

The total should be checked by the cashier against the Cash to Bank figure on the bottom of the Till Contents Sheet.

Date 3 May 2011	bank giro credit		
Cashier's stamp	£50 notes		
	£20 notes	240	00
	£10 notes	60	00
	£5 notes	25	00
Eastern Bank	£2 coins	4	00
Orwell Branch	£1 coins	3	00
	50p & 20p coins	5	10
Account	10p & 5p coins		15
Ashley Supplies	2p and 1p coins		20
Sort Code: 11 16 29	**Total Cash**	337	45
Account Number 82687392	Cheques etc (see overleaf)		
Please do not write or mark below this line	£	337	45

We will now illustrate in a Case Study the whole of the cash handling process explained on the last four pages.

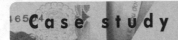

Case study

HESKETH & CO – RECEIVING AND HANDLING CASH

situation

You are employed as assistant cashier for Hesketh & Co. and are responsible for checking receipts from customers. You also have responsibility for checking the cash, completing the necessary documentation and preparing the cash for paying into the bank, using a night safe. The date is 7 September 2011.

You have to carry out the following tasks:

1. You are to calculate the total cash received during the day using the cash sales receipts and enter the total on the Daily Receipts Slip.

2. You are to check the cash float and enter it on the Till Contents Sheet.

3. Complete the Till Contents Sheet and calculate the Cash to Bank figure. Note that:
   - The quantities of notes and coins for cash sales for the day have already been entered on the form.
   - The original float must be retained at the same amount and should consist of the original breakdown of notes and coins.

4. Reconcile (agree) the amount of cash entered on your Daily Receipts Slip with the Cash to Bank figure on the Till Contents Sheet.

5. Prepare a paying-in slip with details of the cash ready for paying in at the bank.

You are provided with the following information and documents:

cash float

The float at the start of 7 September 2011 was £50.00 and consisted of the following notes and coins:

Notes		£
£10 x 1	=	10.00
£5 x 3	=	15.00
Coins		
£2 x 2	=	4.00
£1 x 10	=	10.00
50p x 12	=	6.00
20p x 10	=	2.00
10p x 18	=	1.80
5p x 10	=	0.50
2p x 25	=	0.50
1p x 20	=	0.20
		50.00

cash receipts issued during the day

RECEIPT
Hesketh & C0

Date ___7 September 2011___   No ___K26___

Received from ___T C Yang (cash sales)___

_____

The sum of ___Twenty six pounds___

eighty four pence _____

Cheque		
Cash	26	84

Signed ___J Hesketh_____

WITH THANKS

RECEIPT
Hesketh & C0

Date ___7 September 2011___   No ___K27___

Received from ___Calnan & Co (cash sales)___

_____

The sum of ___Thirty two pounds fifty___

_pence _____

Cheque		
Cash	32	50

Signed ___J Hesketh_____

WITH THANKS

RECEIPT
Hesketh & C0

Date ___7 September 2011___   No ___K28___

Received from ___Ms D Lester (cash sales)___

_____

The sum of ___Eighty nine pounds___

sixty seven pence _____

Cheque		
Cash	89	67

Signed ___J Hesketh_____

WITH THANKS

RECEIPT
Hesketh & C0

Date ___7 September 2011___   No ___K29___

Received from ___May Chen (cash sales)___

_____

The sum of ___One hundred and thirty___

pounds fifty three pence _____

Cheque		
Cash	130	53

Signed ___J Hesketh_____

WITH THANKS

RECEIPT		RECEIPT	
Hesketh & C0		**Hesketh & C0**	

Left Receipt:

Date   7 September 2011   **No**   K30

Received from   White Bros (cash sales)

The sum of   Thirty two pounds seventy pence

Cheque		
Cash	32	70

Signed   J Hesketh

WITH THANKS

Right Receipt:

Date   7 September 2011   **No**   K31

Received from   Trasler Ltd (cash sales)

The sum of   Sixty pounds twelve pence

Cheque		
Cash	60	12

Signed   J Hesketh

WITH THANKS

solution

Task 1

You total up the amount of cash received from the six cash receipts issued and enter the total on the Daily Receipts Slip, as shown below.

DAILY RECEIPTS SLIP

Hesketh & Co

Date   7 September 2011

Total Cash £   372.36

Task 2 solution

You enter the details of the cash float on the Till Contents Sheet (right-hand side) from the data given, producing a total of £50.00.

Note that a colleague has already entered the number of different denominations of notes and coins on the left-hand side of the form. She has not filled in the amounts or worked out the total.

TILL CONTENTS SHEET

Date 7 September 2011			Float		
Notes	**Quantity**	**Total**	**Notes**	**Quantity**	**Total**
£20	12		£20		
£10	6		£10	1	10.00
£5	10		£5	3	15.00
Coins			**Coins**		
£2	7		£2	2	4.00
£1	33		£1	10	10.00
50p	28		50p	12	6.00
20p	22		20p	10	2.00
10p	42		10p	18	1.80
5p	24		5p	10	0.50
2p	55		2p	25	0.50
1p	46		1p	20	0.20
Cash Total			**Float Total**		50.00
			CASH TO BANK		

Task 3 solution

You now complete the Till Contents Sheet (left-hand side) with the value of the notes and coins at the end of the day and add up the Cash Total money column. Your colleague has already entered the number of notes and coins held.

You then deduct the amount of the Float Total from the Cash Total to work out the amount of money which you will be paying into the bank. You enter this figure in the Cash to Bank box.

Task 4 solution

You can now reconcile (agree) the Cash to Bank total of £372.36 with the Daily Receipt Slip total shown on page 71.

TILL CONTENTS SHEET

Date 7 September 2011			Float		
Notes	**Quantity**	**Total**	**Notes**	**Quantity**	**Total**
£20	12	240.00	£20		
£10	6	60.00	£10	1	10.00
£5	10	50.00	£5	3	15.00
Coins			**Coins**		
£2	7	14.00	£2	2	4.00
£1	33	33.00	£1	10	10.00
50p	28	14.00	50p	12	6.00
20p	22	4.40	20p	10	2.00
10p	42	4.20	10p	18	1.80
5p	24	1.20	5p	10	0.50
2p	55	1.10	2p	25	0.50
1p	46	0.46	1p	20	0.20
Cash Total		422.36	**Float Total**		50.00
			CASH TO BANK		372.36

Task 5 solution

You now need to complete the paying-in slip.

But in order to do this you will need to work out what quantities of notes and coins you will have available to make up the total of £372.36.

You will need to refer to the final completed Till Contents Sheet on the previous page.

Taking each complete line in turn, go along the line and work out the amount of money that needs to be paid into the bank, leaving the required amount in the cash float.

For example, on the first line there are 12 x £20 notes = £240. The number of £20 notes required for the float is nil, therefore, all the £20 notes taken during the day ie £240 need to be banked.

The next line shows that 6 x £10 notes (£60) have been taken during the day. Going across the line you will see that only 1 x £10 (£10) is required for the float. Therefore, the amount to be banked will be £60 – £10 = £50 in £10 notes.

This procedure is continued along each line until the paying-in slip is complete (see below):

You then total the paying-in slip, making sure that the total of the paying-in slip equals the Cash to Bank total on the Till Contents List.

The paying-in slip and cash will then be placed in a night safe wallet which will be lodged safely with the bank later in the day, after the bank has closed. It will then be processed by the bank the following day.

Date 7 Sept 2011 — **bank giro credit**

Cashier's stamp

Western Bank
Southbury Branch

Account
Hesketh & Co

Sort Code: 42 73 08
Account Number 22587320

Please do not write or mark below this line

£50 notes		
£20 notes	240	00
£10 notes	50	00
£5 notes	35	00
£2 coins	10	00
£1 coins	23	00
50p & 20p coins	10	40
10p & 5p coins	3	10
2p and 1p coins		86
Total Cash	372	36
Cheques etc (see overleaf)		
£	372	36

CHEQUES

Cheques are issued by banks and building societies to their customers. Payment by cheque is a method of payment used by businesses but it is in decline with personal customers – in fact, some large retail stores now refuse to take them, and there are plans to phase them out by 2018. They are still used, however, for payments made by post, eg payment of bills and payment by business customers for goods and services. A specimen cheque is shown below:

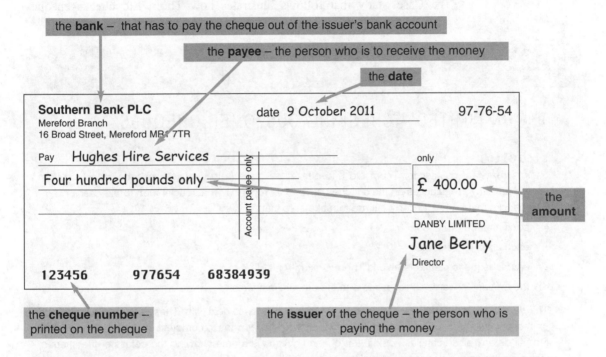

You will see from the above that the business issuing the cheque, which is paying the money is Danby Ltd. The cheque is signed on behalf of the company by one of the directors, Jane Berry. This difference in name is perfectly acceptable as cheques are often signed by someone on behalf of a business and their name may not be the same as the company name.

checking the validity of cheques

When cheques are received by a business it is important to examine them carefully for any irregularities, such as:

- **signature** – has the issuer signed the cheque?
- **payee** – if the name of the payee is not the same as the name of the account into which it is being paid, the cheque will not be accepted by the bank when it is paid in

- **date** – is it out of date (over six months old)? is it post-dated (ie does it have a future date)? – if so, it cannot be paid in (but note that you can fill in a missing date and pay in the cheque)
- **words and figures** – are the money amounts the same?

If no irregularities are found on the cheques then they may be banked. If however, discrepancies are found then these will have to be notified to the supervisor or accounts manager and the cheque returned to the business that issued the cheque.

The Case Study that follows illustrates how Thorn Ltd checks cheques received from its customers.

Case study

THORN LIMITED – CHECKING CUSTOMER CHEQUES

situation

Jack is assistant cashier for Thorn Ltd and one of his tasks is to deal with cheques received from customers. Any irregularities on the cheques have to be reported on a special form to the cashier. The checks that he has to carry out are to make sure that:

- each cheque is signed
- each cheque is in date
- each cheque is made payable to Thorn Limited (or 'Ltd')
- the amount in words corresponds with the amount in figures

The date is 26 April 2011 and Jack has six customer cheques to deal with. These are shown below and on the next two pages. They are followed by the form that Jack has to complete and send to the cashier if he finds any discrepancies. On the left of each cheque is a note showing the details of the cheque, including the date it was received and the invoice it is paying.

Date cheque received:
18 April 2011

Invoice numbers:
375, 376

Cheque value:
£754.40

261258

Southern Bank PLC
116 London Road
Luton, LU2 8JK

date 14 April 2011   42-21-03

Pay Thorn Limited ———————————————— only

Seven hundred and fifty four pounds forty pence   £754.40

Account payee only

PRICE & PARTNERS

D G Parker

261258   422103   47015326

Date cheque received:
21 April 2011

Invoice number:
377

Cheque value:
£132.63

503493

Oak Bank
High Street
Ripon RD3 7KP

date 18 April 2010   20-83-48

Pay Thorn Limited ———————————————— only

One hundred and thirty two pounds 63p ————————   £132.63

Account payee only

I RAFIQ

I Rafiq

503493   208348   37580995

Date cheque received:
25 April 2011

Invoice number:
360

Cheque value:
£74.03

733475

Western Bank PLC
24 The Strand
Plymouth, PL1 5KT

date 20 April 2011   44-78-05

Pay Thorn Limited ———————————————— only

Seventy four pounds thirty pence only ————————   £74.03

Account payee only

FISHER & CO

T S Fisher

733475   447805   94296278

Date cheque received:	Southern Bank PLC	date	21 April 2011	47-82-33

Date cheque received:
25 April 2011

Invoice number:
358

Cheque value:
£110.75

110597

Southern Bank PLC
116 London Road
Luton, LU2 8JK

date _____ 21 April 2011 _____ 47-82-33

Pay   Thorn Limited ————————————————— only

One hundred and ten pounds seventy five pence ——   £110.75

ELDER PRINTING CO

L E Elder

Account payable only

110597   478233   72388942

Date cheque received:
28 April 2011

Invoice number:
380

Cheque value:
£308.62

677582

Oak Bank
High Street
Ripon RD3 7KP

date _____ 22 April 2011 _____ 33-57-02

Pay   Thorn Limited ————————————————— only

Three hundred and eight pounds sixty two pence ——   £308.62

ARDERN SUPPLIES

M Mehta

Account payable only

677582   335702   07673061

---

solution

Jack notices that there are two cheques with discrepancies:

1. The cheque received from I Rafiq is out-of-date (more than 6 months old) – this is probably the customer making an error when writing out the cheque.

2. On the cheque received from T S Fisher the amount in words does not agree with the amount in figures.

Jack must report his findings to the cashier by completing the table as shown below:

Customer	Cheque number	Reason cheque is not valid
I Rafiq	503493	Cheque out of date
Fisher & Co	733475	Amount in words and figures does not agree

OUTSTANDING INVOICE LIST

Businesses need to know exactly how much money is owed to them by their customers at any one time. One of the ways of having this information available is to draw up an **Outstanding Invoice List**. This is a list of customers, with details of the invoices outstanding (the invoice number, the invoice date and the amount owed). When payment is received, details of the payment are entered on the list – these include the date of the payment, the method of payment and whether the payment is valid or not. Note that the method of payment can include BACS and BGC (bank giro credit) as well as cheques. An example of an Outstanding Invoice List is shown below.

OUTSTANDING INVOICE LIST – March 2011

Customer	Invoice number	Invoice date	Amount £	Date payment received	Method of payment	Payment valid Yes/No
K L Cole	460	03.03.11	58.90	04.04.11	Cheque	Yes
E May & Co	464	23.03.11	110.62	19.04.11	Cheque	No
Lawson Ltd	461	10.03.11	73.50	28.04.11	Cheque	Yes
Roche Motors	463	22.03.11	242.78	04.05.11	BGC	Yes
Shepherd Ltd	462	15.03.11	45.20	26.04.11	Cheque	Yes
Wynne Bros	465	29.03.11	217.30	29.04.11	BACS	Yes

	Total £	748.30

The Case Study that follows shows how Jack, who works for Thorn Limited, keeps the Outstanding Invoice List up-to-date, and also how he prepares a paying-in slip for paying the valid cheques into the bank.

THORN LIMITED – OUTSTANDING INVOICE LIST

situation

Jack is also responsible for ensuring the list of outstanding invoices is kept up-to-date by recording the date when a payment is received, by which method, the amount and noting if the payment is valid.

He then completes the paying-in slip by listing the valid cheques and finally takes the cheques together with the paying-in slip to the bank.

His tasks are:

1. Complete the outstanding invoice list dated March 2011 (see next page) as far as possible with the cheques received in the previous Case Study (pages 76-78).

2. Complete the paying-in slip with details of the valid cheques ready for banking. The paying-in slip must only include cheques and should be dated 29 April 2011.

solution

Task 1

The Outstanding Invoice List (see next page) will already have the first four columns filled in. It is Jack's job to complete the right-hand three columns:

*   Date payment received

*   Method of payment

*   Payment valid, yes/no

This data has been entered on the form on the next page.

Note the following points:

*   There are three invoice entries in the list for which a cheque has not been received – there will be no further entry in the form until the payments are received. As we will see in a later Case Study in this chapter, Jack will have to check the bank statement to see if the money has been received by another method of payment, eg BACS or bank giro credit.

*   The cheque for £754.40 from Price & Partners covers two invoices and so the 'Amount' column contains the amount for two individual invoices rather than the total cheque amount.

*   Two of the cheques are not valid and so a 'No' is recorded for these in the final column.

*   Jack therefore has four cheques to pay in at the bank. These will need to be entered on a bank giro credit (see the Task 2 solution on page 82).

OUTSTANDING INVOICE LIST – March 2011

Customer	Invoice number	Invoice date	Amount £	Date payment received	Method of payment	Payment valid Yes/No
Ardern Supplies	380	24.03.11	308.62	28.04.11	Cheque	Yes
Elder Printing Co	358	16.03.11	110.75	25.04.11	Cheque	Yes
Fisher & Co	360	16.03.11	74.03	25.04.11	Cheque	No
Fisher & Co	381	30.03.11	93.14			
Forge Services	378	21.03.11	54.50	15.04.11	Cheque	Yes
Morton's	363	16.03.11	84.80			
Price & Partners	375	17.03.11	392.30	18.04.11	Cheque	Yes
Price & Partners	376	21.03.11	362.10	18.04.11	Cheque	Yes
I Rafiq	377	22.03.11	132.63	21.04.11	Cheque	No
T Wong	356	15.03.11	55.00			
Total £			1,667.87			

Jack will complete these three columns.

Task 2

Jack completes the paying-in slip in two stages as shown below:

1 He first lists the four cheques on the back of the slip with the customer names and amounts and calculates the total.

2 He carries forward the total onto the front of the paying-in slip and enters it twice and enters the current date.

Account				Thorn Ltd	Date		29 April 2011
Cheques					**Cheques**		
					Ardern Supplies	308	62
					Elder Printing Co	110	75
					Forge Services	54	50
					Price & Partners	754	40
					Total carried overleaf £	1,228	27

paying-in slip – back

Date 29 April 2011	bank giro credit		
Cashier's stamp	£50 notes		
	£20 notes		
Western Bank	£10 notes		
Southbury Branch	£5 notes		
	£2 coins		
Account	£1 coins		
Thorn Limited	50p & 20p coins		
	10p & 5p coins		
	2p and 1p coins		
Sort Code: 94 03 50	**Total Cash**		
Account Number 77158671	Cheques etc (see overleaf)	1,228	27
Please do not write or mark below this line	£	1,228	27

paying-in slip – front

OTHER METHODS OF PAYMENT

We have already seen that cheques from customers and cash from sales are commonly paid into the bank account. There are, however, other ways in which payments can be made direct to the bank account. Terms you will come across (and their abbreviations) include:

- Bank Giro Credit (BGC) also known as a Credit Transfer (CT)
- Bankers Automated Clearing Services (BACS)
- Standing Order (SO)
- Direct Debit (DD)
- Clearing House Automated Payments System (CHAPS)

We will describe each of these in turn.

bank giro credit (BGC)

A **bank giro credit** is a slip of paper which is processed through the bank clearing system and is completed by the person making the payment. It is commonly attached as a tear-off slip on credit card and electricity or water bills. If you want to pay the bill you can make a cheque for the payment amount, complete the bank giro credit and pay it through your bank. The giro credit is then processed through the banking system and is paid into the bank account of the organisation receiving the money.

Bank giro credits are also known as CTs, which is short for Credit Transfer. Note that a paying-in slip (see previous page) is also a form of bank giro credit.

Bankers Automated Clearing Services (BACS)

Bankers Automated Clearing Services (BACS) is a computer payment transfer system owned by the banks. It is widely used for regular payments such as insurance premiums, settlement of trade debts, wages and salaries. BACS is a cheap and efficient means of payment because the transfer is set up on a computer file and transferred between the banks' computers – the payment goes direct from account to account.

BACS payments are made in a number of situations:

- by customers who buy from a business regularly settling invoices for variable amounts – all the customer has to do is to set up a **direct credit** payment system with their bank and then instruct the bank in writing (or online) each month the amount to be paid and the date of payment – the bank does the rest through the BACS system and the money is sent automatically to the bank account of the supplier

- by customers paying **standing orders (SO)** (regular payments for the same amount) – the BACS payment is set up with the bank by the person sending the money, for example by a tenant renting office space from a business and paying a regular amount each month

- by bank customers paying **direct debits (DD)** – a regular payment of possibly variable amounts from bank account to bank account where the payment is set up by the business receiving the money, for example an insurance company 'collecting' an insurance premium

Clearing House Automated Payments System (CHAPS)

Clearing House Automated Payments System (CHAPS) – is a computerised system which has been developed to provide same-day fund transfers of large amounts of money.

A CHAPS transfer is set up by the sender of the money who instructs the bank to transfer a sum of money to the recipient's bank account so that it will be available on the same working day. CHAPS transfers are rather expensive to use but they are particularly useful for the sale of and purchase of property and for other large transfers of money.

BANK STATEMENTS

At regular intervals the bank sends out statements of account to its customers or provides them online. A business current account with many items passing through it may have weekly statements, while a less active account or deposit account may have monthly or even quarterly statements.

A specimen bank statement is shown on the next page.

A bank statement sets out columns showing:

- the date of the transaction

- the details of the transaction, followed where appropriate with an abbreviation if the payment is a direct payment, eg BACS (direct credit), DD (direct debit), SO (standing order), BGC (bank giro credit); if the detail is a six digit number, this will normally be the cheque number of a cheque issued by the business

- amounts paid out of the account (debit column) – eg cheques issued, bank charges, standing orders and direct debits

- amounts paid into the account (credit column)

- the running balance of the bank account after each transaction in the 'balance' column – normally starting with the balance from the previous statement

STATEMENT

Mercia Bank
Shrewsbury
SY10 2BQ

Account	Hudson Hall Ltd
Account Number	98494830
Sheet	33
Date	31 May 2011

Date	Details		Debit	Credit	Balance
2011					
1 May	Balance				1,881.60
6 May	J Macmillan Ltd	BACS		561.60	2,443.20
10 May	683002		115.44		2,327.76
13 May	683003		360.00		1,967.76
17 May	Astley Insurance	DD	98.00		1,869.76
18 May	Cash			460.98	2,330.74
20 May	Cheque			511.12	2,841.86
23 May	683005		490.33		2,351.53
24 May	Moore Insurance	SO	160.00		2,191.53
24 May	Cheque			419.75	2,611.28
26 May	683007		180.69		2,430.59
27 May	MacLean & Co	BGC		78.40	2,508.99
31 May	683008		323.70		2,185.29

UPDATING THE OUTSTANDING INVOICE LIST

In the last Case Study of Thorn Ltd (see page 80), Jack had two tasks to complete, one of which was to update the Outstanding Invoice List by entering details of the valid cheques received during the month. If you look at the Outstanding Invoice List on page 81 you will notice that three invoices still remain outstanding:

Fisher & Co	£93.14
Morton's	£84.80
T. Wong	£55.00

The next step in the process is to update the Outstanding Invoice List from the bank statement with any payments that have been received direct to the bank account, eg BACS payments.

If there are still any blank spaces on the Outstanding Invoice List it means that payment for the invoice has not been received and the business may have to chase it up. This process is illustrated in the Case Study which follows.

Case study

THORN LIMITED – UPDATING FROM THE BANK STATEMENT

situation

Jack now has to update the Outstanding Invoice List from the bank statement.

Task 1

Check the bank statement (see the opposite page) and identify any payments received which are shown as outstanding on the Outstanding Invoice List (see page 81).

Task 2

Enter the details of these payments on the Outstanding Invoice List and note any payments that have not yet been received.

solution

Jack examines the bank statement dated 29 April 2011 received by Thorn Ltd and sees that two payments have been paid direct into the bank account:

April 20	Morton's via bank giro credit (BGC)	£84.80
April 29	T Wong via Bankers Automated Clearing Services (BACS)	£55.00

These two payments, which have been received by Thorn Ltd, now need to be entered onto the Outstanding Invoice List by Jack (see page 88).These two payments are shown in bold type for easy identification. This now leaves just one invoice outstanding: Fisher & Co., who owe £93.14.

STATEMENT

Mercia Bank
Shrewsbury
SY10 2BQ

Account	Thorn Ltd
Account Number	77158671
Sheet	14
Date	29 April 2011

Date	Details		Debit	Credit	Balance
2011					
1 Apr	Balance				1,520.70
4 Apr	Cheques			1,270.32	2,791.02
7 Apr	Star Insurance	SO	160.00		2,631.02
11 Apr	Cash			320.54	2,951.56
14 Apr	200459		59.60		2,891.96
18 Apr	R T Telecom	DD	115.00		2,776.96
20 Apr	Morton's	BGC		84.80	2,861.76
22 Apr	200448		241.73		2,620.03
22 Apr	Cash			298.40	2,918.43
26 Apr	Shrewsbury CC	SO	300.00		2,618.43
29 Apr	Cheques			551.18	3,169.61
29 Apr	T Wong	BACS		55.00	3,224.61

OUTSTANDING INVOICE LIST – March 2011

Customer	Invoice number	Invoice date	Amount £	Date payment received	Method of payment	Payment valid Yes/No
Ardern Supplies	380	24.03.11	308.62	28.04.11	Cheque	Yes
Elder Printing Co	358	16.03.11	110.75	25.04.11	Cheque	Yes
Fisher & Co	360	16.03.11	74.03	25.04.11	Cheque	No
Fisher & Co	381	30.03.11	93.14			
Forge Services	378	21.03.11	54.50	15.04.11	Cheque	Yes
Morton's	363	16.03.11	84.80	**20.04.11**	**BGC**	**Yes**
Price & Partners	375	17.03.11	392.30	18.04.11	Cheque	Yes
Price & Partners	376	21.03.11	362.10	18.04.11	Cheque	Yes
I Rafiq	377	22.03.11	132.63	21.04.11	Cheque	No
T Wong	356	15.03.11	55.00	**29.04.11**	**BACS**	**Yes**
Total £			1,667.87			

Chapter summary

- In this chapter we have explained the various ways in which businesses receive payment from their customers including cash, cheques and payments via the bank.

- Guidelines for receiving and handling cash and cheques are described, including the use of a cash float and banking the day's takings on a paying-in slip.

- Various documents are used to record and monitor the receipt of cash and cheque payments; these include the following:
  - Receipt
  - Daily Receipts Slip
  - Till Contents List
  - Table for reporting cheque discrepancies
  - Outstanding Invoice List

- Payments can also be made by the customers of a business direct through the banking system; these include BACS, CHAPS, BGC, CT, SO and DD.

- The bank statement is examined to track and record these incoming direct payments.

Key terms

cash float	an amount of money held by a business to provide a range of change in the cash till at the start of a day's trading
receipt	a document issued by the seller which acknowledges the purchase of goods or services by the customer
daily receipts slip	a form showing the total of cash receipts for the day
till contents list	a form listing the cash float, cash in the till at the end of the day and the amount of cash banked at the end of the day
night safe	a secure wallet used for lodging cash and cheques into the bank outside opening hours
paying-in slip	general term for a form used for paying cash and cheques into a bank account

bank giro credit	a paper slip pre-printed with bank details of a business, used for paying money to an account at a specific bank branch
cheque	a paper form of payment sent by the buyer to settle up what is owed
BACS	Bankers Automated Clearing System is a computer payment system operated by the banks, used for payroll, regular supplier payments, standing orders and direct debits; the term 'BACS payment' it is often used to describe direct credit payments made through BACS
standing order	a series of regular payments set up by the bank customer, using the BACS system
direct debit	a series of BACS payments (which can be variable) set up by the business receiving the money and authorised by the person making the payment
CHAPS	Clearing House Automated Payments System is a computerised system which has been developed to provide same day fund transfers of large amounts of money
bank statement	a copy of a bank account as shown by the banks records provided to the bank customer

Documents for use in these exercises are available at the back of this book, and also as downloads from the Resources section of www.osbornebooks.co.uk

Answers to the asterisked questions are to be found at the back of this book.

4.1* Sarah is a trainee accountant for Grant and Sons. One of her duties is to total up the cash sales for the day and enter the total onto the Daily Receipts List. On pages 91 and 92 you will find the sales receipts for 18 May 2011.

RECEIPT
Grant and Sons

Date   18 May 2011   No 219

Received from   Briggs Services (cash sale)

The sum of   Sixty five pounds and twenty pence

Cheque		
Cash	65	20

Signed   A Grant

WITH THANKS

RECEIPT
Grant and Sons

Date   18 May 2011   No 220

Received from   Poole Trading (cash sale)

The sum of   Forty three pounds and eighty six pence

Cheque		
Cash	43	86

Signed   A Grant

WITH THANKS

RECEIPT
Grant and Sons

Date   18 May 2011   **No** 221

Received from   Marton Cars (cash sale)

The sum of   One hundred and fifty
one pounds and twelve pence

Cheque		
Cash	151	12

Signed   A Grant

WITH THANKS

RECEIPT
Grant and Sons

Date   18 May 2011   **No** 222

Received from   Zhang Stores (cash sale)

The sum of   Thirty three pounds and
fifty pence

Cheque		
Cash	33	50

Signed   A Grant

WITH THANKS

RECEIPT
Grant and Sons

Date   18 May 2011   **No** 223

Received from   Shah Mini-market (cash sale)

The sum of   Twelve pounds and
seventy six pence

Cheque		
Cash	12	76

Signed   A Grant

WITH THANKS

RECEIPT
Grant and Sons

Date   18 May 2011   **No** 224

Received from   Jones Joinery (cash sale)

The sum of   Fifty three pounds and
thirteen pence

Cheque		
Cash	53	13

Signed   A Grant

WITH THANKS

```
┌─────────────────────────────────────────┐
│                                           │
│          DAILY RECEIPTS SLIP              │
│                                           │
│           Grant and Sons                  │
│                                           │
│   Date                                    │
│                                           │
│                                           │
│   Total Cash £                            │
│                                           │
└─────────────────────────────────────────┘
```

Task:

Total up the sales receipts for the day and enter the total onto the Daily Receipts List above.

4.2* You are employed as assistant cashier at Monty's Music Shop and are responsible for checking all receipts from customers. It is also your responsibility to check the cash float and enter the details on the tills contents sheet at the start of each day and bank the takings at the end of the day. All cash received is banked on the day of receipt.

At the start of business on 22 July 2011 the float was £40.00 and consisted of the following notes and coins:

Notes		
2	x	£5.00
Coins		
5	x	£2.00
10	x	£1.00
10	x	0.50p
10	x	0.20p
20	x	0.10p
10	x	0.05p
20	x	0.02p
10	x	0.01p

The sales receipts for the day were as follows:

Receipt No.	Amount
T 52	£108.40
T 53	£32.73
T 54	£51.90
T 55	£124.14
T 56	£26.90
T 57	£13.89

You are required to carry out the following tasks:

Task 1:

Enter the details of the cash float onto the till contents sheet which is shown below.

Task 2:

Calculate the total cash received during the day using the details of the sales receipts (see page 93) and enter the total on the Daily Receipts Slip on page 95.

Task 3:

At the close of business the till is emptied and the cash counted, details of this are shown on the tills contents sheet which you are required to complete.

Task 4:

Monty likes to retain the original float which should consist of the original note and coin analysis for use the following day and bank the remaining cash. Complete the paying-in slip shown on page 95 with the money to be deposited in the night safe at the bank.

TILL CONTENTS SHEET

Date			Float		
Notes	**Quantity**	**Total**	**Notes**	**Quantity**	**Total**
£20	11		£20		
£10	8		£10		
£5	7		£5		
Coins			**Coins**		
£2	9		£2		
£1	31		£1		
50p	14		50p		
20p	16		20p		
10p	24		10p		
5p	13		5p		
2p	28		2p		
1p	15		1p		
Cash Total			**Float Total**		
			CASH TO BANK		

DAILY RECEIPTS SLIP

Monty's Music Shop

Date

Total Cash £

Date_____   bank giro credit

Cashier's stamp

Western Bank
Southbury Branch

Account
Monty's Music Shop

Sort Code: 43 21 85
Account Number 07981534

Please do not write or mark below this line

£50 notes		
£20 notes		
£10 notes		
£5 notes		
£2 coins		
£1 coins		
50p & 20p coins		
10p & 5p coins		
2p and 1p coins		
Total Cash		
Cheques etc (see overleaf)		
£		

4.3 You are employed as assistant cashier for Aztec Toys and are responsible for checking all receipts from customers. It is also your responsibility to check the cash float and enter the details on the tills contents sheet at the start of each day and bank the takings at the end of the day. All cash received is banked on the day of receipt.

At the start of business on 7 December 2011 the float was £45.00 and consisted of the following notes and coins:

Notes		
1	x	£10.00
2	x	£5.00
Coins		
4	x	£2.00
9	x	£1.00
8	x	0.50p
10	x	0.20p
10	x	0.10p
10	x	0.05p
20	x	0.02p
10	x	0.01p

The sales receipts for the day were as follows:

Receipt No.	Amount
301	£46.20
302	£101.75
303	£26.50
304	£83.62
305	£143.40
306	£10.99

You are required to carry out the following tasks:

Task 1:

Enter the details of the cash float onto the till contents sheet which is shown on page 97.

Task 2:

Calculate the total cash received during the day using the details of the sales receipts above and enter the total on the Daily Receipts Slip on page 97.

Task 3:

At the close of business the till is emptied and the cash counted, details of this are shown on the tills contents sheet which you are required to complete and reconcile with the amount of cash entered on your Daily Receipts Slip.

Task 4:

The original float must be retained which should consist of the original note and coin analysis for use the following day the remaining cash must be banked. Complete the paying-in slip shown on page 98 with the money to be deposited in the night safe at the bank.

TILL CONTENTS SHEET					
Date			**Float**		
Notes	**Quantity**	**Total**	**Notes**	**Quantity**	**Total**
£20	15		£20		
£10	7		£10		
£5	6		£5		
Coins			**Coins**		
£2	8		£2		
£1	27		£1		
50p	16		50p		
20p	15		20p		
10p	23		10p		
5p	12		5p		
2p	20		2p		
1p	16		1p		
Cash Total			**Float Total**		
			CASH TO BANK		

DAILY RECEIPTS SLIP

Aztec Toys

Date

Total Cash £

Date_____	bank giro credit		

Cashier's stamp	£50 notes		
	£20 notes		
	£10 notes		
Western Bank	£5 notes		
Southbury Branch	£2 coins		
	£1 coins		
Account	50p & 20p coins		
Aztec Toys	10p & 5p coins		
	2p and 1p coins		
Sort Code: 28 04 35	**Total Cash**		
Account Number 44972067	Cheques etc (see overleaf)		
Please do not write or mark below this line	£		

4.4* You work as an accounts assistant at Electron Games Limited. You have received the three cheques shown below though the post in settlement of customer accounts. Check them carefully and state what is wrong with them. Assume that the date today is 12 October 2011.

(a)

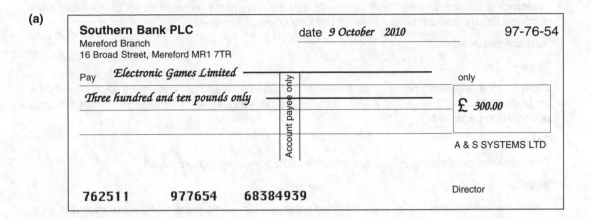

(b)

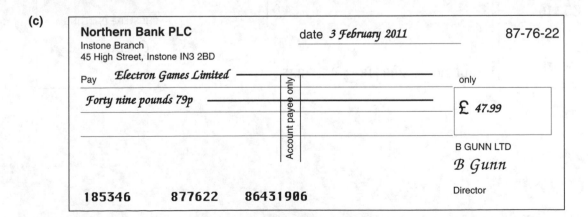

(c)

Northern Bank PLC
Instone Branch
45 High Street, Instone IN3 2BD

date *3 February 2011*

87-76-22

Pay   *Electron Games Limited*

only

Forty nine pounds 79p

£ *47.99*

Account payee only

B GUNN LTD

B Gunn

185346   877622   86431906

Director

4.5* Cedar Associates is a design equipment company and you are employed as their assistant accountant responsible for checking receipts from customers who pay by cheque or through the bank.

Your responsibilities include checking the validity of cheques received and to update the outstanding invoice list with these payments and also payments received direct to the firm's bank account. Finally, you are responsible for banking cheques received.

You are required to:

Task 1:

Carry out the necessary procedures to ensure cheques received from customers which are shown on pages 100 to 102 are valid. If any cheques are not valid, state the reason for this in the table provided on page 102.

Task 2:

Complete the outstanding invoice list on page 103 against cheques received.

Task 3:

Check the bank statement on page 104 and enter any payments received by other methods on to the outstanding invoice list on page 103.

Task 4:

Complete the front and back of the paying-in slip on page 105 with details of valid cheques ready for banking. This paying-in slip must only include cheques and be dated 30 September 2011.

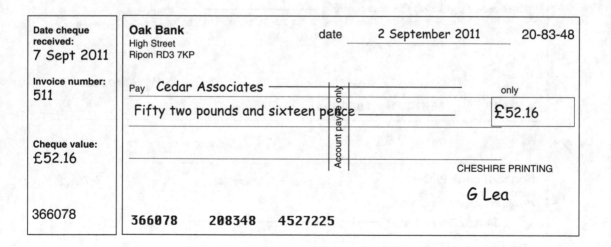

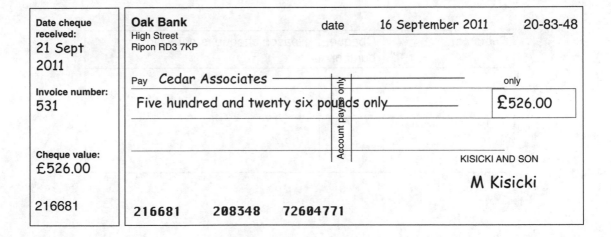

| Date cheque received: | Southern Bank PLC | date 9/9/2011 | 42-21-03 |

Date cheque received:
13 Sept 2011

Invoice numbers:
529

Cheque value:
£315.20

544329

Southern Bank PLC
116 London Road
Luton, LU2 8JK

date 9/9/2011   42-21-03

Pay Cedar Associates   only

Three hundred and fifteen pounds and twenty pence   £315.20

Account payee only

HUANG SERVICES

K Huang

544329   422103   43462110

Date cheque received:
13 Sept 2011

Invoice number:
520

Cheque value:
£76.98

136317

Western Bank PLC
24 The Strand
Plymouth, PL1 5KT

date 9/9/11   32-77-01

Pay Cedar Associates   only

Seventy six pounds eighty nine pence only   £76.98

Account payee only

BEECH & PARTNERS

John Todd

136317   327701   58826678

Date cheque received:
21 Sept 2011

Invoice number:
531

Cheque value:
£526.00

216681

Oak Bank
High Street
Ripon RD3 7KP

date 16 September 2011   20-83-48

Pay Cedar Associates   only

Five hundred and twenty six pounds only   £526.00

Account payee only

KISICKI AND SON

M Kisicki

216681   208348   72604771

Date cheque received: 29 Sept 2011	Southern Bank PLC 116 London Road Luton, LU2 8JK	date	23 Sept 2011	42-21-03

Pay _Cedar Associates_ only

Seventy four pounds and fifty three pence — £74.53

Account payee only

Thompson Ltd

Date cheque received: 29 Sept 2011

Invoice numbers: 534

Cheque value: £74.53

234810

234810   422103   64917749

Date cheque received: 29 Sept 2011

Invoice number: 533

Cheque value: £39.72

217513

Oak Bank
High Street
Ripon RD3 7KP

date   23 September 2011   20-83-48

Pay _Cedar Associates_ only

Thirty nine pounds and seventy two pence £39.72

Account payee only

KISICKI AND SON

M Kisicki

217513   208348   72604771

Customer	Cheque number	Reason cheque is not valid

OUTSTANDING INVOICE LIST – September 2011

Customer	Invoice number	Invoice date	Amount £	Date payment received	Method of payment	Payment valid Yes/No
Beech & Partners	520	03.08.11	76.89			
Beech & Partners	528	05.08.11	133.40			
Cheshire Printing	511	01.08.11	52.16			
Greyfriars Ltd	530	11.08.11	180.60			
Huang Services	529	11.08.11	315.20			
Kisicki & Son	531	15.08.11	526.00			
Kisicki & Son	533	18.08.11	39.72			
Radford Electrics	532	17.08.11	92.51			
Thompson Ltd	534	23.08.11	74.53			
Thompson Ltd	527	10.08.11	163.35			

Total £ 1,654.36

STATEMENT

**Mercia Bank
Shrewsbury
S10 2BQ**

Account	Cedar Associates
Account Number	25101893
Sheet	9
Date	30 September 2011

Date	Details		Debit	Credit	Balance
2011					
1 Sept	Balance				2,350.50
9 Sept	Astbury Ins	DD	301.50		2,049.00
9 Sept	Cash			513.87	2,562.87
12 Sept	620523		184.77		2,378.10
15 Sept	Cheques			1,382.40	3,760.50
16 Sept	Greyfriars	BACS		180.60	3,941.10
19 Sept	S D Telecom	DD	152.00		3,789.10
23 Sept	Cheques			721.00	4,510.10
26 Sept	Shrewsbury CC	SO	350.00		4,160.10
27 Sept	Radford Electrics	BGC		92.51	4,252.61
27 Sept	620524		910.30		3,342.31
28 Sept	620521		46.40		3,295.91
30 Sept	Bank Charges		28.80		3,267.11

Account			Date		
Cheques			Cheques		
			Total carried overleaf £		

Date_____	bank giro credit		
Cashier's stamp	£50 notes		
	£20 notes		
	£10 notes		
Western Bank	£5 notes		
Southbury Branch	£2 coins		
	£1 coins		
Account	50p & 20p coins		
Cedar Associates	10p & 5p coins		
	2p and 1p coins		
Sort Code: 28 03 47	**Total Cash**		
Account Number 62405185	Cheques etc (see overleaf)		
Please do not write or mark below this line	£		

5 Making payments

what this chapter covers . . .

This chapter:

- explains the importance of checking purchase invoices before they are paid to ensure the goods or services received are correct and that all the calculations are accurate

- describes the payment of a purchase invoice using cash

- describes the completion of a cash request slip

- describes the completion of a cheque for payment of a purchase invoice

- explains the use of a remittance advice, which gives details of the payment to the business's suppliers

OCR assessment criteria covered

Unit M3: Making and receiving payments

3.1 Check supporting documents to ensure correct cash payments are made

4.1 Complete a cheque correctly

5.1 Complete a remittance advice

PURCHASE INVOICES

When a business purchases goods or services on credit the supplier sends a purchase invoice setting out the details of the goods or services and their cost. These details identify the supplier and the customer, the items purchased and their price. Invoices were dealt with fully in Chapters 1 and 2.

Remember that there is no actual difference between a sales invoice and a purchase invoice: a sales invoice is a document sent out by your business and a purchase invoice is a document received by your business.

If you receive the purchase invoice below, you are Bedding Supplies and the supplier is Newbon Linen Company.

INVOICE
Newbon Linen Company
Dean House, Parker Street, Nottingham NG4 3BM
Tel 01457 034293 email info@newbonlinen.co.uk
VAT Reg 781 2305 39

Bedding Supplies 26 Lenton Street Nottingham NH4 3BM		invoice number	1734
		purchase order number	217
		date	21 July 2011

Quantity	Product code	Description	Unit price £	Total £
3	KDV	Single Kids Duvet Covers (Boat)	14.95	44.85
6	SNA	Snuggle Throws (Aqua)	10.95	65.70
6	BTN	Bath Towels (Natural)	5.45	32.70
			Sub-total	143.25
			VAT @ 20%	28.65
			Invoice total	171.90

terms:
30 days

INVOICE

Kyle Stationers
72 Terrace Road, Crewe CR2 7HL
Tel 01782 313027 email sales@kylestationers.com
VAT Reg 987 5441 21

Star Sports Ltd
119, Water Street
Crewe
CR2 5JT

invoice number	821
purchase order number	S420
date	1 November 2011

Quantity	Product code	Description	Unit price £	Total £
3	S23	Rolls adhesive tape	0.90	2.70
2	F14	A4 files	2.49	4.98
		Sub-total		7.68
		VAT @ 20%		1.54
Invoice total				9.22

terms:
30 days

CASH REQUEST SLIP

Date   4 November 2011

Supplier   Kyle Stationers

To pay invoice no. 821

Notes	Quantity	Total (£)
£20		
£10		
£5	1	5.00
Coins		
£2	2	4.00
£1		
50p		
20p	1	0.20
10p		
5p		
2p	1	0.02
1p		
Cash Total	£	9.22

solution

You check the invoice from Kyle Stationers and can find no errors, so you make out a cash request slip as shown above, using the least number of notes and coins. This cash will then be used to settle the invoice from Kyle Stationers.

PAYMENT BY CHEQUE

Although payment by cheque is not as popular as it was some years ago it is still a very convenient way of paying for goods or services which have been supplied on credit. Cheque payments made by businesses are sent by post and are often accompanied by a **remittance advice** which sets out what the payment covers. This document is explained on the next page.

We have already explained the format of a cheque in the last chapter and listed the checks that need to be made when a business receives a cheque in payment. A specimen cheque is shown below and the text that follows repeats the main points that have to be observed when writing out a cheque.

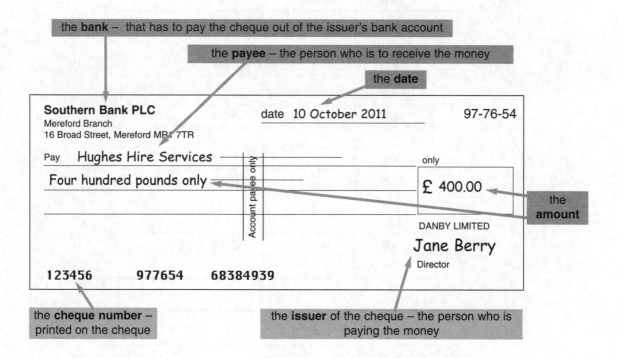

writing out a cheque

When writing out a cheque you should take care to complete the following:

- the correct date
- the name of the payee (the person or business receiving the money)
- the amount in words
- the amount in figures (which should be the same as the amount in words)
- the counterfoil (date, amount, payee) – this is not shown here

No room should be left on the cheque for possible fraudulent additions or alterations; any blank spaces should be ruled through.

If you are working as an assistant you are very unlikely to have authority to sign cheques. There will be senior people, eg managers, partners or directors who have this authorisation and the completed cheque will be passed forward for their approval and signature.

REMITTANCE ADVICE

When payment is made by cheque it is important that the person receiving the cheque has details of the payment so that they know exactly what the payment is for and can allocate it accordingly. Therefore, the remittance advice shows details of the invoices paid, any credit notes and the amount of the accompanying cheque.

If a payment is made by BACS or BGC, the business sends a remittance advice separately to the supplier to enable the payment to be properly allocated against outstanding invoices and any credit notes.

An example of a remittance advice is shown below, with explanations. It will accompany the cheque on the previous page.

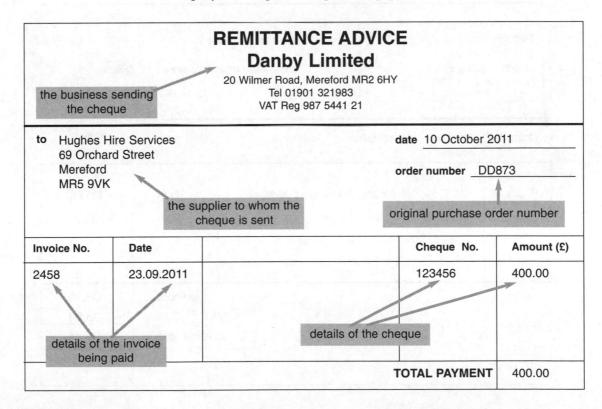

REMITTANCE ADVICE
Danby Limited
20 Wilmer Road, Mereford MR2 6HY
Tel 01901 321983
VAT Reg 987 5441 21

the business sending the cheque

to   Hughes Hire Services
69 Orchard Street
Mereford
MR5 9VK

the supplier to whom the cheque is sent

date 10 October 2011

order number   DD873

original purchase order number

Invoice No.	Date			Cheque No.	Amount (£)
2458	23.09.2011			123456	400.00
				TOTAL PAYMENT	400.00

details of the invoice being paid

details of the cheque

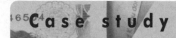

Case study

PILSBURY PRINTING – MAKING PAYMENT BY CHEQUE

situation

Tomas is employed as assistant accountant by Pilsbury Printing. He is responsible for checking purchase invoices prior to payment, making payments by cheque and completing the remittance advices which must accompany all payments made by cheque.

The company has received a purchase invoice from Bond Paper Supplies; this is shown below.

Task

Tomas has to complete a remittance advice note and cheque (and counterfoil) ready for signature and payment of the purchase invoice. Both documents should be dated 24 June 2011.

INVOICE

Bond Paper Supplies

72-76 Mill Street, Bury, BL8 3TW
Tel 0161 583 24732
VAT Reg 843 9124 77

Pilsbury Printing
Unit 10
Heath Trading Estate
Stockport SK4 7BG

invoice number	4108
purchase order number	M523
date	27 May 2011

Quantity	Product code	Description	Unit price £	Total £
6 boxes	X213	Premium A4 Copy paper	18.50	111.00
6 packs	C24	A4 card, 240gsm, assorted	9.20	55.20
			Sub-total	166.20
			VAT @ 20%	33.24
			Invoice total	199.44

terms:
30 days

solution

Tomas completes the remittance advice and cheque as shown below. Note that he has not signed the cheque as he is not authorised to do so.

REMITTANCE ADVICE
Pilsbury Printing

Unit 10, Heath Trading Estate
Stockport SK4 7BG
Tel 0161 979 3256
VAT Reg 123 6124 93

to	Bond Paper Supplies		date	24 June 2011
	72-76 Mill Street,			
	Bury		order number	M523
	BL8 3TW			

Invoice No.	Date		Cheque No.	Amount (£)
4108	27.05.2011		000502	199.44
			TOTAL PAYMENT	199.44

Date 24/06/11

Pay
Bond
Paper
Supplies

£ 199.44

000502

National Bank PLC
Peter Street
Stockport SK3 2LD

Date 24 June 2011

29-32-53

Pay Bond Paper Supplies

One hundred and ninety nine pounds 44p

A/c payee only

£ 199.44

PILSBURY PRINTING

000502   29 32 53   08259301

Chapter summary

- When a purchase invoice is received from a supplier it must be checked carefully before payment can be made. The goods or services invoiced must be correct and the calculations accurate.

- If an invoice is to be paid by cash, a cash request slip should be completed to obtain the correct amount and the appropriate denominations of notes and coins.

- If an invoice is to be paid by cheque the cheque must be completed carefully, making sure that the date, payee, and amount in words and figures are all correct.

- When a cheque payment is sent off by post it will be accompanied by a remittance advice. This document sets out details of the invoice(s) being paid (or any credit notes) and details of the cheque itself.

Key terms

cash request slip   a form used for requesting an amount in cash when a purchase invoice requires to be paid in cash

remittance advice   a document which accompanies a payment to a supplier and gives details of the means of payment and the invoices being paid

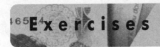

Exercises

Documents for use in these exercises are available at the back of this book, and also as downloads from the Resources section of www.osbornebooks.co.uk

Answers to the asterisked questions are to be found at the back of this book.

5.1* You are employed by Peak Photography as an assistant in their accounts department where you are responsible for checking invoices to ensure that all the calculations are accurate before payment is made.

The invoice shown below has just been received from Jay's Office Supplies and your task is to check the invoice and complete the cash request slip which must list the least possible number of notes and coins. Payment will be made on 25 July 2011.

INVOICE

Jay's Office Supplies
Dean House, 21 Dean Lane, Buxton, BU5 8NU
Tel 01298 54801
VAT Reg 430 7123 50

Peak Photography Market Street Buxton BU5 6TA	
invoice number	227
purchase order number	92
date	20 July 2011

Quantity	Product code	Description	Unit price £	Total £
1	ENL	Packet Envelopes (Large)	3.40	3.40
1	RBA	Box of Assorted Rubber Bands	6.32	6.32
1	RLS	Packet Staples	2.60	2.60
			Sub-total	12.32
			VAT @ 20%	2.46
			Invoice total	14.78

terms:
30 days

CASH REQUEST SLIP

Date _____

Supplier _____

To pay invoice no. _____

Notes	Quantity	Total (£)
£20		
£10		
£5		
Coins		
£2		
£1		
50p		
20p		
10p		
5p		
2p		
1p		
Cash Total		

5.2 As junior cashier for Eagle Computers Ltd one of your tasks is to check purchase invoices received by the company to ensure that all the calculations are accurate. Your responsibility is to pay any invoices where payment is to be made by cash and to complete a cash request slip which is then given to the cashier for payment.

The invoice shown below has just been received from Brock Spares Ltd and your task is to check the invoice and complete the cash request slip which must list the least possible number of notes and coins. Payment will be made on 28 October 2011.

INVOICE

Brock Spares Ltd
Unit 3a, Ashby Industrial Estate, Webb Lane, Durham, DR2 8SD
Tel 01723 401520
VAT Reg 630 5892 36

Eagle Computers Ltd
Princes Street
Durham
DR2 5KP

invoice number	1020
purchase order number	KT394
date	18 October 2011

Quantity	Product code	Description	Unit price £	Total £
3	DP/N	USB Flash Drives	8.95	26.85

Sub-total	26.85
VAT @ 20%	5.37
Invoice total	32.22

terms:
30 days

CASH REQUEST SLIP

Date _____

Supplier _____

To pay invoice no. _____

Notes	Quantity	Total	(£)
£20			
£10			
£5			
Coins			
£2			
£1			
50p			
20p			
10p			
5p			
2p			
1p			
Cash Total			

5.3* Your line manager hands you a statement from Mercia Wholesalers, Unit 12 Riverside Industrial Park, Mereford MR2 7GH with a note indicating the following invoices that are to be paid:

Date	Their Invoice No.	Our Reference	Amount (£)
16 March 2011	5517	C124	765.25
1 April 2011	5792	C172	3,567.80

You are required to complete the remittance advice and cheque ready for signature which are shown below. Both documents should be dated 28 April 2011.

REMITTANCE ADVICE
Nimrod Drainage

Unit 6, Riverside Park, Mereford, MR4 5TF
Tel 01908 761200 Fax 01908 761900
VAT REG GB 0745 8383 46

to   date _____

                                            order number _____

Invoice No.	Date	Cheque No.		Amount (£)
		TOTAL PAYMENT		

Date _____

Pay

National Bank PLC
Mereford Branch
10 Cathedral Street, Mereford, MR1 5DE

Date _____   35-09-75

Pay _____

A/c payee only

£ _____

NIMROD DRAINAGE LIMITED
Director   Director

£ _____

000451   000451   35 09 75   12034875

5.4   Lucy is employed as junior accountant for Presto Supplies and is responsible for checking purchase invoices prior to payment, making payments by cheque and completing remittance advices which must accompany all payments made by cheque.

The company receives a purchase invoice from Wyvern Stationers which is shown below.

Task:

Check the invoice for any errors or discrepancies. Complete the remittance advice note and cheque on the next page ready for signature and payment of the purchase invoice from Wyvern Stationers. Both documents should be dated 30 December 2011.

INVOICE

WYVERN STATIONERS

141 Bell Lane, Wyvern, WY1 4DB
Tel 01905 852013
VAT Reg 781 4304 167

Presto Supplies
18 Fencote Road
Worcester
WR2 6HY

invoice number   12349

purchase order number   10463

date   1 December 2011

Quantity	Product code	Description	Unit price £	Total £
3	LAF9	Lever Arch Files	2.25	6.75
4	D/W	Document Wallets (10 pack)	7.52	30.08
2	DIV	Dividers (10 pack)	5.80	11.60
			Sub-total	48.43
			VAT @ 20%	9.69
			Invoice total	58.12

terms:
30 days

REMITTANCE ADVICE
Presto Supplies

18 Fencote Road, Worcester WR2 6HY
Tel 01905 334482 email: info@prestosupplies.com
VAT REG GB 987 5441 21

to

date _____

order number _____

Invoice No.	Date	Cheque No.	Amount (£)
		TOTAL PAYMENT	

Date _____

Pay

£ _____

126482

Date _____

Southern Bank PLC

Mereford Branch
16 Broad Street, Mereford, MR1 7TR

97-76-54

Pay _____

_____ A/c payee only

_____

£ _____

PRESTO SUPPLIES

126482   97 76 54   34284

6 Source documents for the cash book

what this chapter covers . . .

This chapter:

- introduces the cash book, which is the main bookkeeping record for receipts and payments made in cash and through the bank account

- describes the source documents containing the data required to be entered into the cash book

- illustrates these financial documents including:

  - receipts received and issued

  - cheques received and issued – including cheque counterfoils

- explains how the financial documents are entered into the cash book columns

This chapter is primarily intended as a familiarisation exercise for writing up the cash book, which will be covered in full in the next chapter.

OCR assessment criteria covered

Unit M4: Recording receipts and payments

1.1 Enter receipts and payment details from relevant primary records into the two column analysed cash book

1.2 Enter sales tax (eg VAT)

THE CASH BOOK

an introduction

The layout, operation and balancing of the cash book will be covered in full in the next chapter. But in order that you can appreciate what it looks like and where the entries generated by the documents go, it is illustrated below, together with a few sample entries. Study the layout and read the notes that follow.

cash book: receipts side (debits)　　　　**cash book: payments side (credits)**

Dr					Cash Book				Cr
Date	Details	Cash	Bank	Date	Details	Cheque number	Cash	Bank
2011		£　p	£　p	2011			£　p	£　p
1 Mar	Balances b/d	300.00	550.00	3 Mar	Tombenco	100281		160.00
3 Mar	Cash sales	500.00		4 Mar	Petty cash	100282		100.00
3 Mar	VAT – cash sales	100.00		8 Mar	Insurance	100283		75.00
4 Mar	Cheque R Wilson		3,250.00	9 Mar	Office equipment	100284		1,250.00
				9 Mar	Cash purchases		76.20	
				9 Mar	VAT – cash purchases		15.24	

Notes

- payments received are recorded on the left, and payments made are recorded on the right
- examples of payments received are cash sales (cash kept in the business), and a cheque received from a customer (debtor)
- examples of payments made are:
  - a cheque paid to a supplier
  - cash taken out of the bank to top up the petty cash (see Chapter 10)
  - a cheque issued for expenses (eg insurance)
  - a cheque issued for the purchase of an item used in the business (eg a computer)
- 'Balances b/d' shows the cash and bank balances from the previous period

At this stage you do not need to study the cash book any further. We will now look in detail at the documents which provide the information for the entries.

CASH TRANSACTIONS: RECEIPTS

a note on 'cash' and 'credit'

Business terminology uses the word 'cash' in two ways:

- 'cash' can mean notes and coins – this is what most people understand by the word 'cash'
- a 'cash' transaction can also mean a transaction for 'immediate payment' – as opposed to a 'credit' transaction which means payment can be made at a later date

In this chapter the term 'cash' is mostly used in the first sense – ie using notes and coins.

receipts for cash sales

When a business sells goods or services for cash it may issue a receipt to the buyer, or possibly an invoice marked 'cash sale'. A copy of the document will be kept by the business and used as a source document by the person writing up the receipts (left-hand) side of the cash book.

A cash sales receipt, with sample details, is shown below. Study the receipt and the explanations, and read the notes that follow.

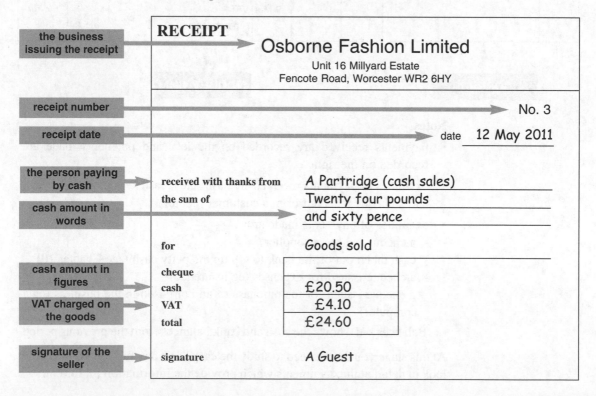

the business issuing the receipt	**RECEIPT**	
	Osborne Fashion Limited	
	Unit 16 Millyard Estate	
	Fencote Road, Worcester WR2 6HY	

receipt number → No. 3

receipt date → date 12 May 2011

the person paying by cash → received with thanks from — A Partridge (cash sales)

cash amount in words → the sum of — Twenty four pounds and sixty pence

for — Goods sold

cheque	—
cash amount in figures → cash	£20.50
VAT charged on the goods → VAT	£4.10
total	£24.60

signature of the seller → signature — A Guest

cash receipt – details needed for the cash book

The details required for the cash book are very simple:

- the date of the receipt – this is the date of the cash sale, ie the date the cash is received by the business
- the amount of cash received

The description of the transaction in the cash book is simply 'Cash Sales', as the name of the customer is not needed.

If the cash sale is subject to VAT then this VAT amount is entered as 'VAT – cash sales' on a separate line underneath 'Cash sales'.

It is possible that if there are a number of cash sales during the day, the amounts will be added up and only the total entered in the cash book. You are not likely, however, to see this in your assignments.

receipts for cash payments

When a business buys goods or services for cash it may receive a receipt (or possibly an invoice) from the supplier. A copy of the document will be kept by the business and used as a source document by the person writing up the cash book.

A sample 'cash purchases' receipt is shown below.

The details entered in the cash book are similar to the details taken from a cash sales receipt – date, description 'cash purchases' and amount – but they are entered on the payments side of the cash book. Again, if the purchase is subject to VAT then this VAT amount is entered as 'VAT – cash purchases' on a separate line underneath 'Cash purchases'. Study the example and explanations shown below.

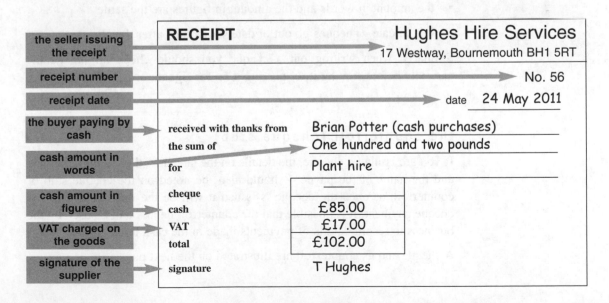

CREDIT TRANSACTIONS: CHEQUES RECEIVED

The receipts on the last two pages have been for **cash** sales and purchases – cash (notes and coins) has been used, and payment is immediate.

As we have already seen, many business transactions are on **credit** – the sale or purchase takes place, an invoice is issued, and payment is made later. Payment may be made through the BACS or with a **cheque**.

A business may deal with cheques in a number of situations:

- a business receives cheques from customers in settlement of accounts

- a business writes cheques when paying suppliers

- a business writes cheques when paying expenses (eg wages and electricity bills) and when paying for items purchased (eg computers)

- a business writes a cheque when drawing (taking) cash out of the bank, eg to top up the petty cash imprest

This chapter focuses on dealing with cheques received from customers settling accounts and cheques issued to pay suppliers.

checking the cheque

When receiving a cheque from a customer, you should always check that:

- it is signed

- it is made payable to the correct person or business

- the amount in words and the amount in figures are the same

- it is in date – cheques go out of date six months after the cheque date

Similarly, when writing out a cheque you should check all the details carefully before signing it, or passing it on for signature.

the counterfoil (cheque stub)

If you are issuing a cheque, the details on the cheque – the amount, the date and the name of the payee – should also be noted on the cheque stub or counterfoil, as once the cheque is issued it will be the main record of the cheque payment. It is possible that the counterfoil details will be used by the business to record details of payments made in the cash book.

A cheque and its counterfoil are illustrated on the next page.

We will now deal with the practical issues of receiving cheques from customers.

DEALING WITH CHEQUES FROM CUSTOMERS

When you are writing up the cash book, you will need to record the receipt of cheques from customers. In addition to the name of the customer and the amount received you will need to record the date it is going to be banked. Look at the example below.

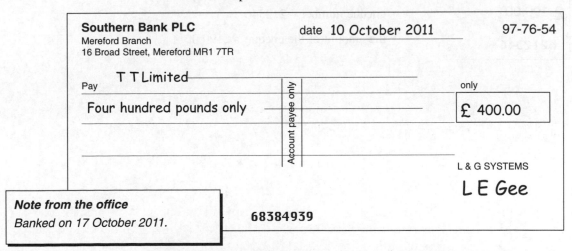

The details that go into the cash book (left-hand 'receipts' side) are:

- the date the cheque is banked – 17 October 2011
- name of the customer – L & G Systems – into 'Details' column
- the amount of £400 is entered in the bank column

DEALING WITH CHEQUES ISSUED

When you write up the cash book, you need to record details of cheques issued by your business to suppliers, for expenses and for other purchases. The details are:

- the date the cheque has been written out

- the name of the payee (the person to whom the cheque is payable)

- the cheque number

- the amount of the cheque, ie the amount paid

These details are normally written on the cheque counterfoils, as in the example shown below. These act as a record of the payment made.

7 Oct 2011

To

G M Hopkins

CREDITOR

£ 190.00

212346

example

Here payment is made to G M Hopkins, a supplier and creditor (a 'creditor' is a person or organisation to whom the business owes money). The details that go into the cash book (right-hand 'payments' side) are:

- the date the cheque is issued – 7 October 2011

- the name of the supplier (creditor) – G M Hopkins (note that the word 'CREDITOR' appears on the cheque counterfoil)

- cheque number – 212346

- the amount of the cheque – £190.00

Chapter summary

- The cash book is the bookkeeping record which shows cash received and paid out by a business and transactions through the bank account.
- The cash book is written up from financial documents processed by the business.
- Financial documents for money received include:
    - receipts for cash sales made to customers
    - cheques received from customers for credit sales
- Financial documents for money paid out include:
    - receipts issued by suppliers for cash purchases made
    - cheques (or cheque counterfoils) for payments made to suppliers, for expenses and for the purchase of other items
- Details to be entered in the cash book include:
    - date of the transaction
    - details of the transaction
    - amount of the cheque/receipt

Key terms

cash payment	can mean both notes and coins and immediate payment
credit payment	payment made at a later date than the sale or purchase
counterfoil	cheque 'stub' which records the details of the cheque, ie date, amount and payee

**Exercises**

Cash book pages for use in these exercises are available at the back of this book, and also as downloads from the Resources section of www.osbornebooks.co.uk

Answers to the asterisked questions are to be found at the back of this book.

6.1* You work for Osborne Fashion Ltd. You are to list the details (including the date) that will be recorded in the company's cash book (receipts side) from the documents on the next three pages. The two money columns are:

– cash

– bank

You can use (or photocopy) the following table for your answer

Cash Book (receipts side)

Date	Details	Cash £ p	Bank £ p

Copies of cash receipts to customers

(a)

RECEIPT

Osborne Fashion Limited
Unit 16 Millyard Estate
Fencote Road, Worcester WR2 6HY

No. 3

date 12 May 2011

received with thanks from A Partridge (cash sales)

the sum of Twenty four pounds

and sixty pence

for Goods sold

cheque	——
cash	£20.50
VAT	£4.10
total	£24.60

signature A Guest

(b)

RECEIPT

Osborne Fashion Limited
Unit 16 Millyard Estate
Fencote Road, Worcester WR2 6HY

No. 4

date 13 May 2011

received with thanks from J Singh (cash sales)

the sum of Thirty six pounds

and 84p

for Goods sold

cheque	——
cash	£30.70
VAT	£6.14
total	£36.84

signature A Guest

Cheques received by Osborne Fashion Ltd

(c)

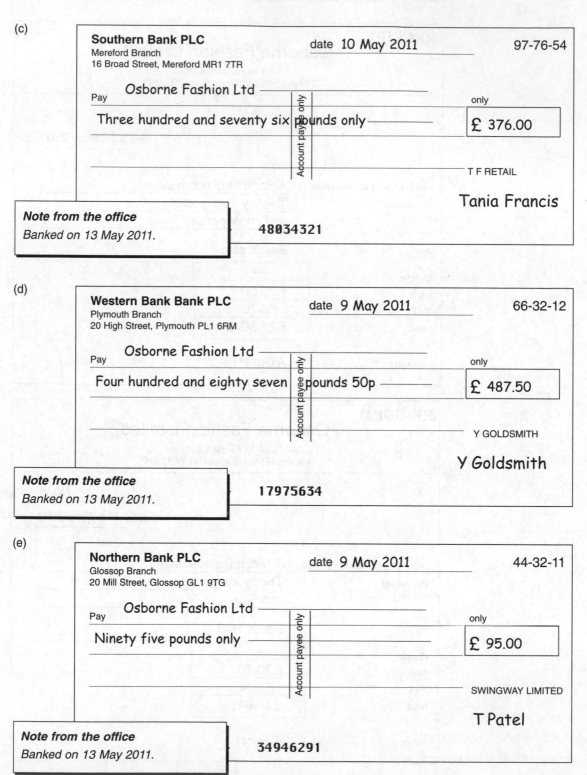

Southern Bank PLC
Mereford Branch
16 Broad Street, Mereford MR1 7TR

date 10 May 2011   97-76-54

Pay   Osborne Fashion Ltd

Three hundred and seventy six pounds only   only

£ 376.00

Account payee only

T F RETAIL

Tania Francis

Note from the office
Banked on 13 May 2011.   48034321

(d)

Western Bank Bank PLC
Plymouth Branch
20 High Street, Plymouth PL1 6RM

date 9 May 2011   66-32-12

Pay   Osborne Fashion Ltd

Four hundred and eighty seven pounds 50p   only

£ 487.50

Account payee only

Y GOLDSMITH

Y Goldsmith

Note from the office
Banked on 13 May 2011.   17975634

(e)

Northern Bank PLC
Glossop Branch
20 Mill Street, Glossop GL1 9TG

date 9 May 2011   44-32-11

Pay   Osborne Fashion Ltd

Ninety five pounds only   only

£ 95.00

Account payee only

SWINGWAY LIMITED

T Patel

Note from the office
Banked on 13 May 2011.   34946291

(f)

Wyvern Bank PLC
Worcester Branch
30 Deansway, Worcester WR1 7GG

date 10 May 2011   99-22-10

Pay   Osborne Fashion Ltd   only

One hundred and ninety six pounds only   £ 196.00

Account payee only

TRENDTIME

Emma Troon

Note from the office
Banked on 13 May 2011.   92494121

(g)

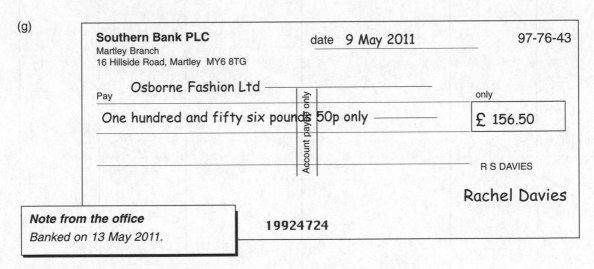

Southern Bank PLC
Martley Branch
16 Hillside Road, Martley MY6 8TG

date 9 May 2011   97-76-43

Pay   Osborne Fashion Ltd   only

One hundred and fifty six pounds 50p only   £ 156.50

Account payee only

R S DAVIES

Rachel Davies

Note from the office
Banked on 13 May 2011.   19924724

(h)

Wyvern Bank PLC
Worcester Branch
30 Deansway, Worcester WR1 7GG

date 10 May 2011   99-22-10

Pay   Osborne Fashion Ltd   only

Ninety seven pounds 50p only   £ 97.50

Account payee only

PATRICIA SMITH

P Smith

Note from the office
Banked on 13 May 2011.   28720183

6.2* You are working for Osborne Fashion Ltd and are required to list the details (including the date) that will be recorded in the cash book (payments side) from the documents on the next three pages. The three columns are:

– cheque number

– cash

– bank

Remember to record the cheque numbers next to the supplier names in the first column.

You can use (or photocopy) the following table for your answer:

Cash Book (payments side)

Date	Details	Cheque Number	Cash £ p	Bank £ p

Copies of cash receipts from suppliers

(a)

RECEIPT	Hermes Car Hire
	17 Chepstow Way
	Bromswich B17 8GH

No. 103

date   24 May 2011

received with thanks from   Osborne Fashion (cash purchases)

the sum of   Ninety pounds only

for   Peugeot 307 hire

cheque	——
cash	£75.00
VAT	£15.00
total	£90.00

signature   K Singh

(b)

RECEIPT	Ludlow Leather
	17 Tenbury Way
	Ludlow SY6 8VF

No. 76

date   25 May 2011

received with thanks from   Osborne Fashion (cash purchases)

the sum of   Twenty four pounds only

for   4 x leather belts @ £6

cheque	——
cash	£20.00
VAT	£4.00
total	£24.00

signature   R Marchant

(c)

RECEIPT	ACJ Fashions

ACJ Fashions
3 Nansen Road
Stockport ST1 5FG

No. 121

date   25 May 2011

received with thanks from   Osborne Fashion (cash purchases)
the sum of   Twelve pounds only

for   4 × pairs black tights @ £3.00

cheque	——
cash	£10.00
VAT	£2.00
total	£12.00

signature   A C Jones

Payments to suppliers (creditors)

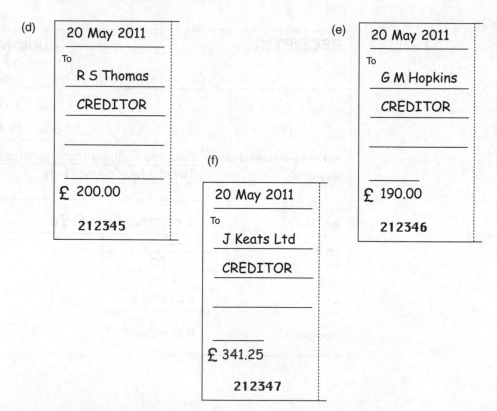

(d)

20 May 2011

To
R S Thomas

CREDITOR

£ 200.00

212345

(e)

20 May 2011

To
G M Hopkins

CREDITOR

£ 190.00

212346

(f)

20 May 2011

To
J Keats Ltd

CREDITOR

£ 341.25

212347

(g)

| 20 May 2011 |
| To |
| R Graves & Co |
| CREDITOR |
| £380.00 |
| **212348** |

(h)

| 20 May 2011 |
| To |
| W Owen |
| CREDITOR |
| £ 245.95 |
| **212349** |

(i)

| 20 May 2011 |
| To |
| W Blake Ltd |
| CREDITOR |
| £71.25 |
| **212350** |

(j)

| 23 May 2011 |
| To |
| T Hughes |
| CREDITOR |
| £ 76.00 |
| **212351** |

(k)

| 23 May 2011 |
| To |
| T Hardy |
| Insurance |
| CREDITOR |
| £140.40 |
| **212352** |

(l)

| 23 May 2011 |
| To |
| S Plath & |
| Associates |
| CREDITOR |
| £ 195.00 |
| **212353** |

7 Writing up and balancing the cash book

what this chapter covers . . .

This chapter:

- explains in further detail the layout of the cash book and the entries made into the cash and bank columns

- shows details of cash and cheques received and paid in

- shows details of payments made by cash and cheque

- shows how the columns of the cash book are balanced and describes the significance of the balances

- explains the role and duties of the cashier

There are fully worked Case Studies which show how a variety of transactions are entered into the cash book by the cashier and are balanced off at the end of the month.

OCR assessment criteria covered

Unit M4: Recording receipts and payments

1.1 Enter receipts and payment details from relevant primary records into the two column analysed cash book

1.2 Enter sales tax (eg VAT)

1.3 Total, balance and cross check the cash book

INTRODUCTION TO THE CASH BOOK

One of the most important books of account kept by firms is the **cash book**. As we saw in the last chapter, the cash book contains records of money received and payments made out of the business, including both cash and bank (cheque, bank giro credit, and other bank transfers) transactions. It is important to keep the cash book up to date since it enables the owner(s) of the business to know how much money the business has in cash and at the bank at any moment of time.

In addition to the cash book many firms also keep a **petty cash book** to record small items of expenditure such as the purchase of postage stamps and incidental expenses. The petty cash book is dealt with in Unit M5 Maintaining Petty Cash Records (see Chapters 9 – 11).

USES AND PURPOSE OF THE CASH BOOK

a cash and bank book

The cash book is used to record both the cash and bank transactions in one book. Some students may find the name "cash book" confusing in that it contains both cash and bank transactions so why not call it the cash/bank book? However, in accounting terms it has always been known as the cash book.

The cash book is used to record the money aspect of bookkeeping transactions such as:

- **cash transactions**

    - all receipts in cash

    - most payments for cash, except for small value expense payments (which as mentioned above are paid through the petty cash book)

- **bank transactions**

    - all receipts through the bank (including payment of cash into the bank)

    - all payments through the bank (including the withdrawal of cash from the bank)

purposes of the cash book

The activities of businesses involve cash or bank transactions at some point. The entry of these transactions into the cash book is carried out by the cashier, who is responsible for maintaining and controlling the cash book.

One of the main purposes of the cash book is to maintain a record of the amount of money held in cash and the bank balance at any point in time.

Another purpose of maintaining a cash book is to keep a permanent record of money received and payments made into and out of a business. It is important to note that any transaction entered into the cash book must be supported by documentary evidence such as an invoice, statement or receipt.

THE ROLE OF THE CASHIER

The cashier has the important role of maintaining and controlling the money coming into and going out of a business and providing up-to-date information on the organisation's cash position at any time. The cashier's duties and responsibilities include the following:

- issuing receipts for cash (and sometimes cheques) received
- recording receipts for cash and bank transactions (cheques and bank giro credits)
- making authorised payments in cash and by cheque against documents received (such as invoices and statements) showing amounts due
- recording payments by cash, cheque or bank transfers
- paying cash and cheques received into the bank
- issuing cash to the petty cashier who operates the firm's petty cash book (see Chapters 9 – 11)
- controlling the firm's cash, using a secure cash till or cash box
- checking the accuracy of the cash and bank balances at regular intervals

the importance of accuracy and security

With so many transactions being entered into the cash book, the cashier must ensure that the accounting procedures are followed at all times. These involve:

- **Accuracy** – making sure each transaction is entered correctly in the cash book. The entry should normally be in strict date order using the correct date, description and amount. Any payment made must be supported by the correct documentation and be properly authorised.

  At intervals, usually one month, the cash book is checked against the bank statement and a bank reconciliation statement prepared (this is dealt with in the next chapter). It is therefore important to ensure that all entries made in the cash book are accurate and all additions correct to enable the reconciliation to be made quickly and efficiently.

- **Security** – the cash box and the cheque books must be kept in a safe and secure place. It is also important to ensure all payments have been correctly authorised before payment is made.

- **Confidentiality** – it is important that all information contained in the cash book is kept confidential and not revealed to unauthorised people or organisations. This includes details of individual entries and the cash and bank balances of the organisation.

LAYOUT OF THE CASH BOOK

There are a number of cash book layouts that may be used by a business. For your assessment, however, you are required to use a two column cash book, as illustrated below. Note that the cash book is divided into two sides. The left-hand side is the **Receipts** side in which all receipts are entered, and the right-hand side is the **Payments** side where all the payments are recorded.

cash book: receipts side (debits)   **cash book: payments side (credits)**

Dr									Cash Book		Cr
Date	Details	Cash	Bank	Date	Details	Cheque number	Cash	Bank
2011		£ p	£ p	2011			£ p	£ p
1 Mar	Balances b/d	300.00	550.00	3 Mar	Tombenco	100281		160.00
3 Mar	Cash sales	500.00		4 Mar	Petty cash	100282		100.00
3 Mar	VAT – cash sales	100.00		8 Mar	Insurance	100283		75.00
4 Mar	Cheque R Wilson		3,250.00	9 Mar	Office equipment	100284		1,250.00
				9 Mar	Cash purchases		76.20	
				9 Mar	VAT – cash purchases		15.24	

money in   **money out**

the receipts side of the cash book

The left-hand side of the cash book is the debit side in which all the receipts are entered. You may like to refer to the debit side as the "in" side where all the monies received "into" the business will be entered. As can be seen from the illustration of the cash book above, there are two money columns on the debit (left-hand) side:

- cash
- bank

In the column headed "cash" all cash receipts into the business (but not into the bank) are entered and in the "bank" column all the money paid into the bank (eg cheques, cash, bank giro credits, standing orders, direct debits received) are entered.

the payments side of the cash book

The right-hand side of the cash book is the credit side where all the payments are entered. Again, you may find it useful to refer to the credit side as the "out" side where all the payments "out of" the business are recorded. Again, there are two money columns on this side of the cash book for cash and bank.

In the column headed "cash" all cash payments "out of" the business are entered and in the "bank" column all bank payments (eg cheques, cash withdrawals, standing orders, direct debits paid) are entered. In the column headed 'Cheque Number' the cheque number relating to the payment is entered.

Read through and study the two Case Studies that follow. One deals with the receipts side of the cash book, the other with the payments side. You will see that these are the two processes introduced in the last chapter.

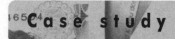

Case study

ACE ADVERTISING AGENCY:
WRITING UP THE CASH BOOK – RECEIPTS SIDE

situation

Kulvinder is assistant cashier at Ace Advertising Agency. One of Kulvinder's tasks is to bank any cash and cheques received and enter them in the cash book. On the following pages (145-147) you will find details of cash receipts (including VAT where appropriate) and cheques received during June 2011.

Kulvinder is asked to enter the receipts in the cash book. This is shown on page 147.

Notes:

*   The first entry in the cash book is 'Balances b/d'. This is the amount of cash held by the business and the balance of the bank account at the beginning of June. We will deal with balancing these accounts later in the chapter.

*   The amounts then entered in the cash book are the amounts of the various cheques and the cash sales (including VAT where appropriate).

Cheques received by Ace Advertising Agency

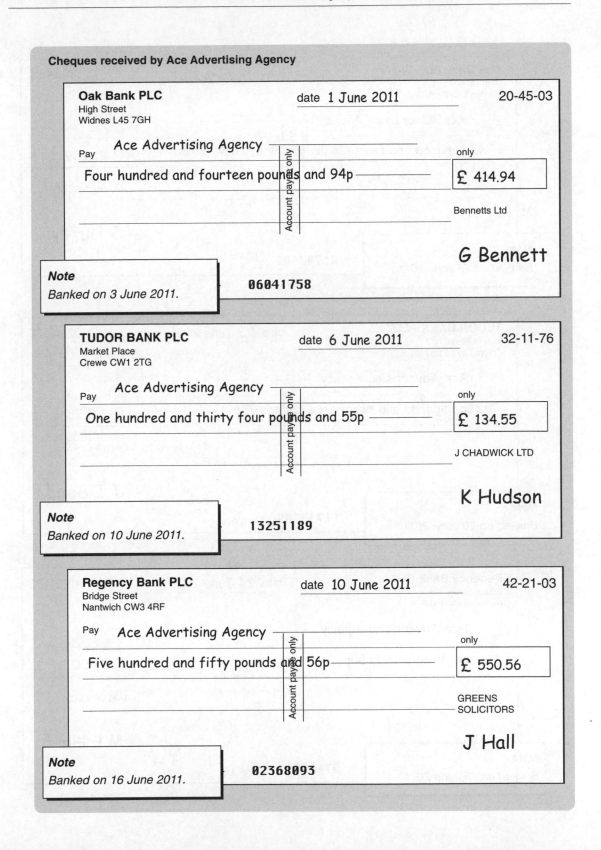

Oak Bank PLC
High Street
Widnes L45 7GH

date 1 June 2011

20-45-03

Pay Ace Advertising Agency

Four hundred and fourteen pounds and 94p

only

£ 414.94

Bennetts Ltd

G Bennett

Account payee only

Note
Banked on 3 June 2011.

06041758

TUDOR BANK PLC
Market Place
Crewe CW1 2TG

date 6 June 2011

32-11-76

Pay Ace Advertising Agency

One hundred and thirty four pounds and 55p

only

£ 134.55

J CHADWICK LTD

K Hudson

Account payee only

Note
Banked on 10 June 2011.

13251189

Regency Bank PLC
Bridge Street
Nantwich CW3 4RF

date 10 June 2011

42-21-03

Pay Ace Advertising Agency

Five hundred and fifty pounds and 56p

only

£ 550.56

GREENS
SOLICITORS

J Hall

Account payee only

Note
Banked on 16 June 2011.

02368093

Oak Bank PLC
High Street
Widnes L45 7GH

date 17 June 2011

20-45-03

Pay   Ace Advertising Agency

Account payee only

only

Two hundred and fourteen pounds ninety nine pence ———

£ 214.99

MARSH MOTORS

S Duffy

Note
Banked on 23 June 2011.

01782481

TUDOR BANK PLC
Market Place
Crewe CW1 2TG

date 23 June 2011

32-11-76

Pay   Ace Advertising Agency

Account payee only

only

Three hundred and twenty one pounds 75p ———

£ 321.75

Owen & Owen

J I Bond

Note
Banked on 28 June 2011.

11733409

Regency Bank PLC
Bridge Street
Nantwich CW3 4RF

date 24 June 2011

42-21-03

Pay   Ace Advertising Agency

Account payee only

only

Ninety three pounds 50p ———

£ 93.50

TAYLORS LTD

M E Hart

Note
Banked on 29 June 2011.

57483841

ACE ADVERTISING AGENCY
RECEIPT

No. 167

date 9 June 2011

received from   Joe Kirk (cash sales)

the sum of   Fifty one pounds 48p

for   Goods supplied

cheque	—
cash	£42.90
VAT	£8.58
total	£51.48

signature   K Patel

**Copies of cash
receipts to customers**

ACE ADVERTISING AGENCY
RECEIPT

No. 168

date 30 June 2011

received from   Anna Hopkins (cash sale)

the sum of   Forty four pounds 76p

for   Goods supplied

cheque	—
cash	£37.30
VAT	£7.46
total	£44.76

signature   K Patel

**The cash book, showing
entries for the cheques
and receipts**

Dr								Cr
				Ace Advertising Agency: Cash Book				
Date	Details	Cash	Bank	Date	Details	Cheque number	Cash	Bank
2011		£ p	£ p	2011			£ p	£ p
1 Jun	Balances b/d	200.00	750.00					
3 Jun	Bennetts Ltd		414.94					
10 Jun	J Chadwick Ltd		134.55					
16 Jun	Greens Solicitors		550.56					
23 Jun	Marsh Motors		214.99					
28 Jun	Owen & Owen		321.75					
29 Jun	Taylors Ltd		93.50					
9 Jun	Cash sales	42.90						
9 Jun	VAT – cash sales	8.58						
30 Jun	Cash sales	37.30						
30 Jun	VAT – cash sales	7.46						

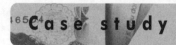

Case study

ACE ADVERTISING AGENCY: WRITING UP THE CASH BOOK – PAYMENTS SIDE

situation

One of Kulvinder's tasks as accounts assistant is to prepare a schedule of payments to suppliers (creditors) due at the end of the month.

Kulvinder will also make cash payments in respect of cash purchases made during the month.

payments to creditors

The payments due to suppliers (creditors) at the end of April are shown below. Kulvinder's job is to prepare the cheques for payment and complete the counterfoils. She will then enter the payments into the credit side of the cash book. The next cheque number is 404520.

Name of supplier	Amount Due	Usual payment terms
Halls Ltd	£148.20	Net monthly
Business Supplies Co.	£325.70	Net monthly
Frank Osborne Ltd	£85.41	Net monthly
White Office Supplies	£113.30	Net monthly
A1 Electrics Ltd	£390.00	Net monthly
Eco Printing	£85.00	Net monthly

Kulvinder then writes out the cheques to the suppliers on the due date of 30 June.

The six cheque book counterfoils (cheque stubs) that she has made out are shown on the next page.

Note that the names of the suppliers are shown and marked 'CREDITOR' (a creditor is a person or organisation that is owed money).

payments for cash purchases

Kulvinder also deals with any cash purchases made during the month and enters the details (including VAT if applicable) in the cash book on the credit side. Details of cash purchases are shown on page 150.

payments to creditors

30 June 2011

To

Halls Limited

CREDITOR

£148.20

404520

---

30 June 2011

To

Business

Supplies Co.

CREDITOR

£325.70

404521

---

30 June 2011

To

Frank

Osborne Ltd

CREDITOR

£ 85.41

404522

---

30 June 2011

To

White Office

Supplies

CREDITOR

£113.30

404523

---

30 June 2011

To

A1 Electrics Ltd

CREDITOR

£390.00

404524

---

30 June 2011

To

Eco Printing

CREDITOR

£ 85.00

404525

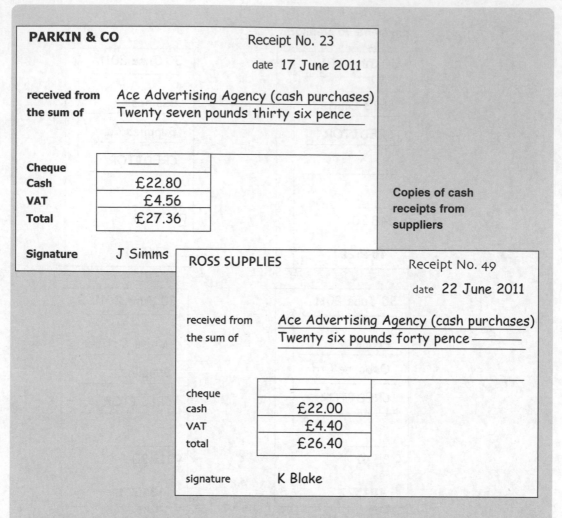

PARKIN & CO   Receipt No. 23

                                date 17 June 2011

received from   Ace Advertising Agency (cash purchases)
the sum of   Twenty seven pounds thirty six pence

Cheque	———
Cash	£22.80
VAT	£4.56
Total	£27.36

Copies of cash receipts from suppliers

Signature   J Simms

ROSS SUPPLIES   Receipt No. 49

                                date 22 June 2011

received from   Ace Advertising Agency (cash purchases)
the sum of   Twenty six pounds forty pence ———————

cheque	———
cash	£22.00
VAT	£4.40
total	£26.40

signature   K Blake

Kulvinder then writes the details for all the cheques and cash purchases in the cash book on the 'payments' side (right-hand side), as shown opposite. All the details she needs for all of the columns will be taken from the cheque counterfoils.

Notes

- When entering the cheques in the cash book it is important to include the cheque number, this makes the payment easier to identify when checking the cash book against the bank statement.

- When entering a payment to a creditor in the cash book, it is the name of the creditor that is entered in the Details column.

- When entering cash purchases, enter the VAT applicable to the purchase on a separate line.

Dr				Ace Advertising Agency: Cash Book				Cr
Date	Details	Cash	Bank	Date	Details	Cheque number	Cash	Bank
2011		£ p	£ p	2011			£ p	£ p
1 Jun	Balances b/d	200.00	750.00	30 Jun	Halls Ltd	404520		148.20
3 Jun	Bennetts Ltd		414.94	30 Jun	Business Supplies Co	404521		325.70
10 Jun	J Chadwick Ltd		134.55	30 Jun	Frank Osborne Ltd	404522		85.41
16 Jun	Greens Solicitors		550.56	30 Jun	White Office Supplies	404523		113.30
23 Jun	Marsh Motors		214.99	30 Jun	A1 Electrics Ltd	404524		390.00
28 Jun	Owen & Owen		321.75	30 Jun	Eco Printing	404525		85.00
29 Jun	Taylors Ltd		93.50	17 Jun	Cash purchases		22.80	
9 Jun	Cash Sales	42.90		17 Jun	VAT – cash purchases		4.56	
9 Jun	VAT – cash sales	8.58		22 Jun	Cash purchases		22.00	
30 Jun	Cash sales	37.30		22 Jun	VAT – cash purchases		4.40	
30 Jun	VAT – cash sales	7.46						

Entries for payments received

BALANCING THE CASH BOOK

The cash book contains the accounts for cash and bank transactions and needs to be balanced at regular intervals. The business will then know the amount of cash held by the business and have an estimate of the amount of money in the bank.

The debit (receipts) and credit (payments) sides of the cash book include columns for bank and cash transactions.

Illustrated on the next page is the cash book of Attwood Limited showing the transactions for the first week in April. As you will see there are entries in all the money columns, and at the end of the week they have all been totalled. In addition the cash and bank columns have been **balanced**.

Study the format and then read the explanation that follows. Note that the grey arrows and boxes below have been added to help with the explanation. They do not appear in the actual cash book.

cash book: receipts side (debits)   **cash book: payments side (credits)**

Dr						Attwood Limited: Cash Book				Cr
Date	Details	Cash	Bank		Date	Details	Cheque number	Cash	Bank
2011		£	£		2011			£	£
4 Apr	Balances b/d	300	1,550		5 Apr	E Lee & Co	616001		160
5 Apr	Cash sales	200			6 Apr	Hayes Ltd	616002		200
5 Apr	VAT – cash sales	40			6 Apr	S Crane	616003		145
6 Apr	Mango Designs		98		7 Apr	Cash purchases		100	
6 Apr	John Mason & Associates		205		7 Apr	VAT – cash purchases		20	
7 Apr	J Jones		76		8 Apr	R Jameson	616004		282
7 Apr	R Singh		94		8 Apr	S Maverick	616005		70
8 Apr	D Whiteman Ltd		45						
8 Apr	Natasha Barclay and Co		110						
					8 Apr	Balances c/d		420	1,321
		540	2,178					540	2,178
9 Apr	Balances b/d	420	1,321						

the balancing figure, ie the difference between the debit and credit total is entered on the side of the lower total – this is the 'balance'

totals box

balance brought down for the following week

=

balance carried down from this week

balancing the cash and bank columns

The cash and bank columns are balanced as follows:

step 1 Add up the figures in all the cash and bank columns and make a separate note of the totals.

step 2 Compare the totals of the cash columns – they are £540 and £120.

step 3 Take away the lower figure from the higher to give the *balance* of the cash remaining (£540 – £120 = £420).

step 4 Write down the *higher* of the two totals at the bottom of *both* cash columns in a totals 'box' (£540).

step 5 The balance of cash remaining (£420) is entered as a balancing item *above* the totals box on the side which gave the lower total, ie the credit (right-hand) side. This £420 is written down again (brought down) below the cash total on the *other* side, the debit (left-hand) side as the opening balance for next week (£420).

step 6   The two bank columns are dealt with in the same way: £2,178 is the higher of the two column totals and is entered in the totals box on both sides, the balance is the difference between the subtotals, ie

£2,178 − £857 = £1,321 (the balance of money in the bank)

This is entered above the totals box in the bank column which had the lower initial total, in this case the credit side.

Note that in the cash book shown on the previous page the cash and bank balances have been **brought down** on the debit (left-hand) side, which indicates a positive bank balance. It is very important to appreciate that the bank columns of the cash book represent the firm's own records of bank transactions and the balance at the bank, but the bank statement may well show different figures. The next chapter explains how to reconcile the two figures.

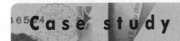

Case study

GEE TRADING COMPANY CASH BOOK: A WORKED EXAMPLE

situation

Anton is employed by The Gee Trading Company as a cashier.

Set out below are the receipts and payments that require entering in the firm's cash book for the week commencing 2 May 2011. The completed cash book is shown on the next page.

2011

1 May	Balances at start of week: cash £150.00, bank £1,200.00.
3 May	Received a cheque from J Kirk, a debtor, for £136.50.
3 May	Received a cheque from Peak Products Ltd, a debtor, £421.00.
3 May	Paid C. Wager, a creditor, £80.00 by cheque no. 201334.
4 May	Paid for purchases in cash £42.00 plus VAT £8.40.
4 May	Received £64.00 cash into the business from cash sales, including VAT of £10.66.
5 May	Paid Lee & Sons, a creditor, £133.60 by cheque no. 201335.

5 May   Received £54.00 cash into the business from cash sales including VAT of £9.00.

5 May   Cashed cheque for £81.70 (no. 201336) at bank to reimburse petty cashier to top up petty cash imprest.

6 May   Received cheque from Albert Brown Ltd for £298.35.

6 May   Paid £125.00 to Ace Products, a creditor, cheque no. 201337.

6 May   Paid cash £20.00 donation to local charity (no VAT).

7 May   Received cheque from D Patel for £210.60.

7 May   Paid cheque to D Hunt Ltd, a creditor, £72.00, cheque no. 201338.

On 7 May Anton has to balance off the cash book and bring down the balances.

solution

Anton writes up and balances the cash book :

Dr						Gee Trading Company:Cash Book			Cr
Date	Details	Cash £ p	Bank £ p	Date	Details	Cheque Number	Cash £ p	Bank £ p
2011				2011				
1 May	Balances b/d	150.00	1,200.00	3 May	C Wager	201334		80.00
3 May	J Kirk		136.50	4 May	Cash purchases		42.00	
3 May	Peak Products Limited		421.00	4 May	VAT – cash purchases		8.40	
4 May	Cash sales	53.34		5 May	Lee & Sons	201335		133.60
4 May	VAT – cash sales	10.66		5 May	Petty cash	201336		81.70
5 May	Cash sales	45.00		6 May	Ace Products	201337		125.00
5 May	VAT – cash sales	9.00		6 May	Donation		20.00	
6 May	Albert Brown Limited		298.35	7 May	D Hunt Limited	201338		72.00
7 May	D Patel		210.60	7 May	Balance c/d		197.60	1,774.15
		268.00	2,266.45				268.00	2,266.45
8 May	Balance b/d	197.60	1,774.15					

balancing the cash columns

The cash columns are balanced as follows:

- Add up all the cash receipts (including the opening balance) in the cash column on the receipts ("in") side (and note the total):
  £150.00 + £53.34 + £10.66 + £45.00 + £9.00 = £268.00

- Add up all the cash payments in the cash column on the payments ("out") side (and note the total):
  £42.00 + £8.40 + £20.00 = £70.40

- From the total cash receipts (the higher figure) deduct the total cash payments (the lower figure): £268.00 − £70.40 = £197.60

- The difference of £197.60 represents the cash left over at the end of the period, and is the 'balance' of the cash account.

- This balance of £197.60 is entered on the credit (payments) side of the cash book as 'Balance c/d' which stands for 'balance carried down'. The cash columns are then totalled off at the end of the period, producing a total on both sides of £268.00. The balance of £197.60 is then entered again on the debit (receipts) side of the cash book (on the line below the totals) as 'Balance b/d' which stands for 'balance brought down'.

- This means that the opening balance on 8 May 2011 is £197.60, the amount of cash which the firm is holding at the beginning of the next period.

balancing the bank columns

The bank columns are balanced off in exactly the same way:

- Add up all the bank receipts in the bank column on the receipts ('in') side:

  £1,200.00 + £136.50 + £421.00 + £298.35 + £210.60 = £2,266.45

- Add up all the bank payments in the bank column on the payments ('out') side:

  £80.00 + £133.60 + £81.70 + £125.00 + £72.00 = £492.30

- Deduct the lower figure from the higher figure:

  £2,266.45 − £492.30 = £1,774.15

- The difference of £1,774.15 represents the amount of money in the firm's bank account at the end of the period according to our records, this is known as the 'balance'.

- The balance of £1,774.15 is entered at the bottom of the bank column which had the lower total, as 'Balance c/d'. In this case the bank column is on the credit (right-hand) side of the cash book.

- The bank columns are then added up, and should produce the same total of £2,266.45.

- The bank balance 'Balance c/d' (£1,774.15) is then entered again on the debit (receipts) side of the cash book as 'Balance b/d' which stands for 'balance brought down'.

- This means that the opening bank balance on 8 May 2011 is £1,774.15, the amount of money in the bank account, according to the firm's records, which it has available for the beginning of the next period.

note

It is possible that when you balance the bank columns the bank 'balance b/d' is on the opposite 'payments' side of the cash book. This means that the business has a bank overdraft. This is explained in the next Case Study.

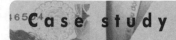

Case study

GEE TRADING COMPANY GOES OVERDRAWN

situation

If a business spends more than it receives through the bank account, the result is a bank overdraft. In other words, the business will be borrowing from the bank.

If in the Case Study on the previous pages, Gee Trading Company issued a cheque to C. Wager for £2,080.00 instead of £80.00, the effect would be to increase the total of the bank payments by £2,000. The effect on the cash book would be:

- Total receipts would still be £ 2,266.45, but . . .

- Total payments are now £2,080.00 + £133.60 + £81.70 + £125.00 + £72.00 = £2,492.30.

- Total payments of £2,492.30 less total receipts £2,266.45 = £225.85 (ie the business has paid out more than it has received)

- The balancing figure of £225.85 is entered above the total box on the debit (left-hand) side as 'balance c/d' and then on the credit (right-hand) side as 'balance b/d'. This represents a bank overdraft of £225.85.

The amended cash book is shown below.

Dr				Gee Trading Company:Cash Book				Cr
Date	Details	Cash £ p	Bank £ p	Date	Details	Cheque Number	Cash £ p	Bank £ p
2011				2011				
1 May	Balances b/d	150.00	1,200.00	3 May	C. Wager	201334		2,080.00
3 May	J Kirk		136.50	4 May	Cash purchases		42.00	
3 May	Peak Products Limited		421.00	4 May	VAT – cash purchases		8.40	
4 May	Cash sales	53.34		5 May	Lee & Sons	201335		133.60
4 May	VAT – cash sales	10.66		5 May	Petty cash	201336		81.70
5 May	Cash sales	45.00		6 May	Ace Products	201337		125.00
5 May	VAT – cash sales	9.00		6 May	Donation		20.00	
6 May	Albert Brown Limited		298.35	7 May	D Hunt Limited	201338		72.00
7 May	D Patel		210.60	7 May	Balance c/d		197.60	
7 May	Balance c/d		225.85					
		268.00	2,492.30				268.00	2,492.30
8 May	Balance b/d	197.60		8 May	Balance b/d			225.85

The rule is therefore:

- bank balance on the debit (left-hand) side = money in the bank

- bank balance on the credit (right-hand) side = bank overdraft (money owed)

Chapter summary

- A cash book is maintained to record both cash and bank transactions on a regular basis, for example, once a month, so that the business can assess its financial position.

- The role of the cashier is vital in assessing the financial position since his/her duties include recording the money coming into the business and the money going out. After entering the various receipts and payments he/she will calculate the amount of cash held by the business and the bank balance.

- When entering transactions in the cash book it is important to ensure that items are entered accurately and confidentiality is maintained at all times. The cash and the cheque books should be kept in a secure place.

- The cash book layout used in this chapter follows that used by many businesses. The layout incorporates both receipts and the payments.

- The cash book is balanced on a regular basis. The cash account will always show a positive (debit) balance, but the bank account balance may be either on the debit side of the cash book (money in the bank) or on the credit side (a bank overdraft).

Key terms

cash book	a record of cash and bank transactions, over a period of time, which tells the business how much cash it has and what its bank balance is
cashier	the person in a business responsible for maintaining and controlling the money that flows into and out of a business; this role is important because the cashier provides up-to-date information about the business cash position at any point
overdraft	borrowing from the bank on the bank account, (shown in the cash book as a credit balance, brought down on the right-hand side)

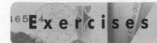

Exercises

Blank cash book pages are printed after each question and also at the end of this book. They may also be downloaded from www.osbornebooks.co.uk

Answers to the asterisked questions are to be found at the back of this book.

7.1* Andrew works as an assistant in the accounts department of Shaw Products Limited, which uses a two column cash book. One of Andrew's tasks is to bank receipts from cash sales and any cheques received during the month and enter the details in the cash book. On 1 October 2011, he had opening balances of £136.12 in the cash account and £1,206.10 in the bank account.

Tasks:

1   Enter the opening balances.

2   Enter details of receipts (including VAT where appropriate) received by the company during October 2011 using the documents on pages 158-160.

Cheques received by Shaw Products Limited

Oak Bank PLC
High Street
Widnes L45 7GH

date 4 October 2011   20-45-03

Pay   Shaw Products Ltd   only

Two hundred and sixty pounds only   £ 260.00

Account payee only

Rose Services

P Rose

Note
Banked on 7 October 2011.

02970318

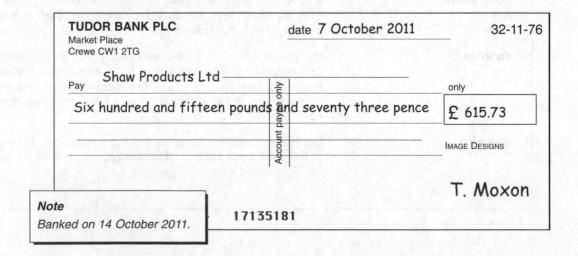

TUDOR BANK PLC
Market Place
Crewe CW1 2TG

date 7 October 2011   32-11-76

Pay   Shaw Products Ltd   only

Six hundred and fifteen pounds and seventy three pence   £ 615.73

Account payee only

IMAGE DESIGNS

T. Moxon

Note
Banked on 14 October 2011.

17135181

Regency Bank PLC
Bridge Street
Nantwich CW3 4RF

date 11 October 2011

42-21-03

Pay Shaw Products Ltd

One hundred and forty one pounds 20p

Account payee only

only

£ 141.20

Pollard Products

E Jilstone

Note
Banked on 14 October 2011.

68930179

Oak Bank PLC
High Street
Widnes L45 7GH

date 13 October 2011

20-45-03

Pay Shaw Products Ltd

Four hundred and seventeen pounds 38p

Account payee only

only

£ 417.38

Yung Wong & Co

B. Yung

Note
Banked on 21 October 2011.

08432175

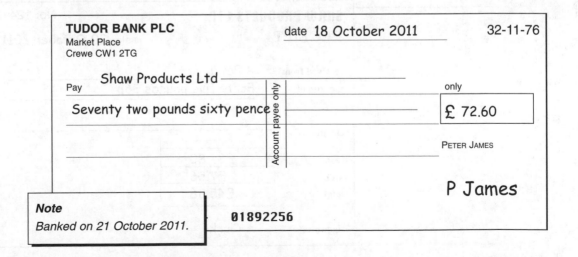

TUDOR BANK PLC
Market Place
Crewe CW1 2TG

date 18 October 2011

32-11-76

Pay Shaw Products Ltd

Seventy two pounds sixty pence

Account payee only

only

£ 72.60

PETER JAMES

P James

Note
Banked on 21 October 2011.

01892256

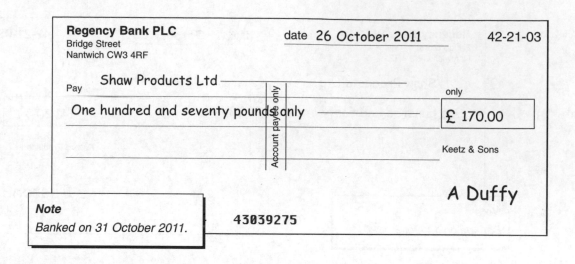

Regency Bank PLC
Bridge Street
Nantwich CW3 4RF

date 26 October 2011   42-21-03

Pay   Shaw Products Ltd ─────────────

Account payee only   only

One hundred and seventy pounds only ───────   £ 170.00

Keetz & Sons

A Duffy

Note
Banked on 31 October 2011.

43039275

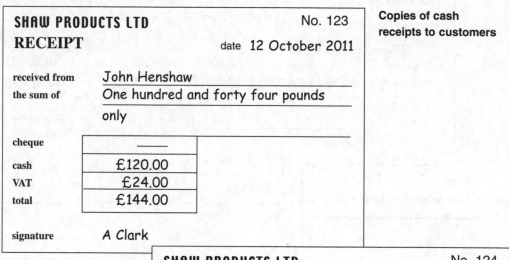

SHAW PRODUCTS LTD   No. 123
RECEIPT   date 12 October 2011

received from   John Henshaw
the sum of   One hundred and forty four pounds
                    only

cheque	───	
cash	£120.00	
VAT	£24.00	
total	£144.00	

signature   A Clark

**Copies of cash
receipts to customers**

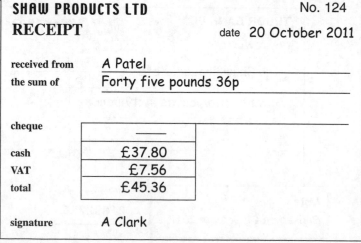

SHAW PRODUCTS LTD   No. 124
RECEIPT   date 20 October 2011

received from   A Patel
the sum of   Forty five pounds 36p

cheque	───	
cash	£37.80	
VAT	£7.56	
total	£45.36	

signature   A Clark

Cash Book – Shaw Products

Date	Details	Cash £ p	Bank £ p		Date	Details	Cheque Number	Cash £ p	Bank £ p

7.2* Sarah has just been appointed assistant accountant for a small publishing company, Clover Designs. One of Sarah's tasks is to enter all payments made by cheque and any cash purchases in the company's two column cash book.

During May 2011 the company pays several of its creditors by cheque and Sarah also makes some cash purchases on behalf of the company.

Task:

Enter details of payments using the documents shown on pages 162-164.

Copies of cheque counterfoils

13 May 2011 To Charles Edge Ltd CREDITOR £521.30 **508921**	13 May 2011 To May & Co. CREDITOR £79.40 **508922**	13 May 2011 To M Singh Ltd CREDITOR £721.80 **508923**
31 May 2011 To Taylor Bros. CREDITOR £ 92.75 **508924**	31 May 2011 To Bond Paper Co CREDITOR £201.50 **508925**	31 May 2011 To Wang Stationers CREDITOR £ 57.33 **508926**

Note

A blank cash book page is reproduced on page 164. You may photocopy this page.

Blank forms are also available for download from the Resources section of www.osbornebooks.co.uk

Copies of cash receipts from suppliers

KERR PRODUCTS	No. 177
RECEIPT	date 11 May 2011

received from Clover Designs (Cash purchases)

the sum of One hundred and forty two pounds

fifty six pence

cheque	——
cash	£118.80
VAT	£23.76
total	£142.56

signature J E Kerr

J S SUPPLIES LTD	No. 84
RECEIPT	date 24 May 2011

received from Clover Designs (Cash purchases)

the sum of Twenty nine pounds 47p

cheque	——
cash	£24.56
VAT	£4.91
total	£29.47

signature C Nettel

Cash Book – Clover Designs

Date	Details			Cash £ p	Bank £ p

Date	Details		Cheque Number	Cash £ p	Bank £ p

7.3* As cashier for Spencer's Office Supplies your task is to maintain the firm's two column cash book. Below are the details of the receipts and payments of cash and bank for the month of March 2011.

1 Mar   Opening balances of cash in hand £235.00 and balance at bank £2,345.00 (Dr).

3 Mar   Cash purchases £40.00 plus VAT £8.00.

4 Mar   Received cheques from the following customers:

Peak Dental Practice £44.85

Rippon (Estate Agents) £79.00

9 Mar   Received cheque from Premier Garage £144.25, a customer.

11 Mar   Cash purchases £17.90 plus VAT £3.58.

11 Mar   Cash sales – £92.30 plus VAT £18.46 received into the business.

15 Mar   Paid Office Supplies Ltd, a creditor, £750.75 cheque no. 925001.

16 Mar   Paid a creditor, Cox & Co, by cheque no. 925002, £550.00.

18 Mar   Received cheque from Halls Ltd, a customer, £106.00.

25 Mar   Cash sales – £67.00 plus VAT £13.40 received into the business.

25 Mar   Paid K Marsh, a creditor, £110 by cheque no. 925003.

30 Mar   Received cash sales £123.00 plus VAT £24.60 into the business.

30 Mar   Paid Lomas Bros, a creditor, £400 by cheque no. 925004.

31 Mar   Cash sales £82.60 plus VAT £16.52.

You are required to

(a)   Enter the opening balances.

(b)   Enter the details of receipts and payments (including VAT where appropriate) in the cash book.

(c)   Total and balance the cash book and bring down the balance.

Cash Book – Spencer's Office Supplies

Date	Details	Cash £	Bank £	Cheque Number	Details	Date	Cash £ p	Bank £ p

7.4   Firbank & Worrall run a haulage company in Cheshire. Their cashier, Roger, is responsible for the company's two column cash book. Roger is asked to write up the cash book for June 2011 from the following details:

1 Jun	Balances brought down:	Cash Account £205.00 (Dr)
		Bank overdraft £733.20 (Cr)

2 Jun   Received cheque from Mr Wilshaw, a customer, £129.00.

3 Jun   Bought purchases for cash £132.00 plus VAT £26.40.

6 Jun   Received cheque from Browns Products, a creditor, for £1,340.00.

7 Jun   Cash sales £135.00 plus VAT £27.00.

8 Jun   Paid cheque to Ace Insurance (a creditor) £300.00, cheque no. 511615.

9 Jun   Cheque 511616 for £85.00 cashed at bank, for petty cash imprest top up.

10 Jun   Received cheque from Akhash Foods £419.25.

14 Jun   Paid the following creditors by cheque:

Bowman Products	£300.00	Cheque no. 511617
Goddard Ltd	£ 75.00	Cheque no. 511618
Pete's Garage	£ 526.00	Cheque no. 511619

17 Jun   Bought purchases for cash £26.00 plus VAT £5.20.

23 Jun   Received cheque from K Green, a customer, £600.00.

24 Jun   Cash sales £80.00 plus VAT £16.00 received into the business.

27 Jun   Paid K. White £1,254.00 by cheque no. 511620.

28 Jun   Received cheque £421.00 from Polar Foods Ltd.

You are required to

(a)   Enter the opening balances.

(b)   Enter the details of receipts and payments (including VAT where appropriate) as shown above, in the cash book.

(c)   Total and balance the cash book and bring down the balance.

Cash Book – Firbank & Worrall

Date	Details	Cheque Number	Cash £ p	Bank £ p

Date	Details	Cash £ p	Bank £ p

7.5 Julie Capper has recently opened a new business called 'Capper's Crafts'. It sells craft and art materials to schools and retail shops.

Julie has appointed Jo to help her with the book-keeping side of the business. One of Jo's tasks is to enter the daily transactions into the business's two column cash book.

At the beginning of March 2011 the following balances were brought down:

  Cash in hand   £252.00

  Balance of money in the bank £1,300.00

Documentation relating to all the transactions involving the receipt and payment of money during March 2011 are shown on the next seven pages:

You are required to carry out the following tasks

(a) Enter the opening balances.

(b) Enter details of receipts using the documents shown on pages 170 to 173.

(c) Enter details of payments using the documents shown on pages 174 to 176.

(d) Total and balance the cash book and bring down the balance.

Important note

Ensure that you enter all the transactions in each task in strict date order. This may mean that the entries in the cash book are not in date order. This does not pose a problem, and is acceptable practice.

cheques received by Capper's Crafts

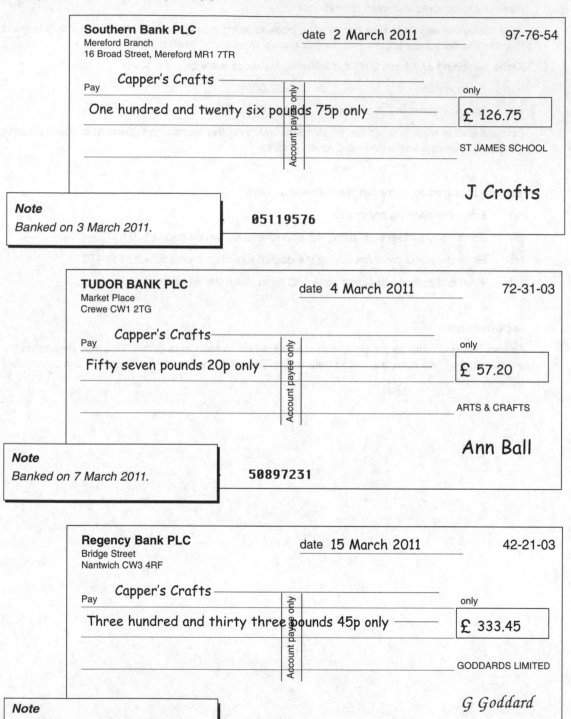

Southern Bank PLC
Mereford Branch
16 Broad Street, Mereford MR1 7TR

date 2 March 2011

97-76-54

Pay Capper's Crafts

One hundred and twenty six pounds 75p only

only

£ 126.75

ST JAMES SCHOOL

J Crofts

Account payee only

Note
Banked on 3 March 2011.

05119576

TUDOR BANK PLC
Market Place
Crewe CW1 2TG

date 4 March 2011

72-31-03

Pay Capper's Crafts

Fifty seven pounds 20p only

only

£ 57.20

ARTS & CRAFTS

Ann Ball

Account payee only

Note
Banked on 7 March 2011.

50897231

Regency Bank PLC
Bridge Street
Nantwich CW3 4RF

date 15 March 2011

42-21-03

Pay Capper's Crafts

Three hundred and thirty three pounds 45p only

only

£ 333.45

GODDARDS LIMITED

G Goddard

Account payee only

Note
Banked on 16 March 2011.

71178604

cheques received by Capper's Crafts

OAK BANK PLC
High Street
Widnes L45 7GH

date 18 March 2011   20-45-03

Pay Capper's Crafts _____ only

Two hundred and twenty five pounds only ——————

£ 225.00

Account payee only

BEECH PRIMARY SCHOOL

J Higgins

46852266

> **Note**
> *Banked on 22 March 2011.*

TUDOR BANK PLC
Market Place
Crewe CW1 2TG

date 24 March 2011   32-11-76

Pay Capper's Crafts _____ only

One hundred and fifteen pounds only ——————

£ 115.00

Account payee only

HOBBY CRAFT CO

M T Low

98470456

> **Note**
> *Banked on 25 March 2011.*

Regency Bank PLC
Bridge Street
Nantwich CW3 4RF

date 29 March 2011   42-21-03

Pay Capper's Crafts _____ only

Sixty three pounds only ——————

£ 63.00

Account payee only

MELLORS LIMITED

R Mellor

92735041

> **Note**
> *Banked on 30 March 2011.*

receipts issued by Capper's Crafts for cash sales

CAPPER'S CRAFTS	No. 101
RECEIPT	date 7 March 2011

received from T Ahmed

the sum of Fifty one pounds only

for Goods supplied

cash	£42.50
VAT	£8.50
total	£51.00

signature Jo Dunn

CAPPER'S CRAFTS	No. 102
RECEIPT	date 10 March 2011

received from Banks Lane School

the sum of Seventy four pounds forty pence

for Goods supplied

cash	£62.00
VAT	£12.40
total	£74.40

signature Jo Dunn

receipts issued by Capper's Crafts for cash sales

CAPPER'S CRAFTS	No. 103
RECEIPT	date 14 March 2011

received from   Judith's Art Materials

the sum of   Ninety one pounds twenty pence

for   Goods supplied

cash	£76.00
VAT	£15.20
total	£91.20

signature   Julie Capper

CAPPER'S CRAFTS	No. 104
RECEIPT	date 24 March 2011

received from   Worrall's Workshop

the sum of   Twenty seven pounds and sixty pence

for   Goods supplied

cash	£23.00
VAT	£4.60
total	£27.60

signature   Jo Dunn

cash receipts issued by Capper's Crafts' suppliers

DOBBY ARTS & CRAFTS   No. 27

RECEIPT   date   4 March 2011

received from   Capper's Crafts

the sum of   Two hundred and ninety two pounds fifty
                  pence

for   Cash purchases

cash	£243.75
VAT	£48.75
total	£292.50

signature   E Firth

BURGESS SUPPLIES   No. 201

RECEIPT   date 15 March 2011

received from   Capper's Crafts

the sum of   Twenty one pounds 24p

for   Cash purchases

cash	£17.70
VAT	£3.54
total	£21.24

signature   Mary Grainger

PATEL WHOLESALE   No. 89

RECEIPT   date 31 March 2011

received from   Capper's Crafts

the sum of   Thirty three pounds only

for   Cash purchases

cash	£27.50
VAT	£5.50
total	£33.00

signature   D P A Patel

cheque counterfoils written out by Capper's Crafts

2 March 2011
To
Star
Services
CREDITOR
£50.00
123466

4 March 2011
To
G. Noone & Co
CREDITOR
£98.40
123467

7 March 2011
To
K Ashworth
CREDITOR
£ 232.05
123468

11 March 2011
To
Akbar's
Wholesale
CREDITOR
£ 409.50
123469

17 March 2011
To
Business
Supplies
CREDITOR
£37.50
123470

22 March 2011
To
Rushton Ltd
CREDITOR
£ 108.20
123471

8 Bank reconciliation statements

This chapter:

- deals with differences between the balance of the bank accounts in the cash book and the closing balance of the bank account shown by the bank statement for the same period.

- explains these differences which are shown in a document known as a 'Bank Reconciliation Statement', which lists the following:
  1. items which are in the cash book but not on the bank statement
  2. items which are on the bank statement but not in the cash book

- explains the importance of this process which enables the business to update its cash book and helps prove the accuracy of the bookkeeping of the business and the bank.

OCR assessment criteria covered

Unit M4: Recording receipts and payments

2.1 Check individual items on the bank statement against the cash book

2.2 Update the cash book from the bank statement

2.3 Prepare a bank reconciliation statement

THE NEED FOR AN ACCURATE CASH BOOK

As we saw in the last two chapters, most organisations keep a record of their cash and bank transactions in a cash book. The cash book contains a record of both the cash account and the bank account and shows the balance in each account at the end of a period. When the cash book has been balanced off it is usual to check the details with the records of the firm's bank transactions as recorded by the bank, ie the bank statement.

To enable this check to be made the cashier will need to ensure that the cash book is completely up-to-date and a recent bank statement has been obtained from the bank.

Often, when a comparison is made between the bank balance as shown in the firm's cash book with that shown on the bank statement, the two balances will be different. It is for this reason that a **bank reconciliation statement** is prepared to **reconcile** ('tally up') the two balances. Differences normally result from cheques written out and not yet paid in or paying in slips not yet banked. Differences can also result from simple errors.

An example of a bank reconciliation statement is shown below. As you can see, it is a very straightforward calculation. The process of drawing up a bank reconciliation statement will be explained in full on pages 183-187.

	£	£
CECILIA WHOLESALE LIMITED		
Bank Reconciliation Statement as at 31 October 2011		
Balance at bank as per Cash Book		525
Add: unpresented cheques		
Taverner Trading Company	60	
Puccini Partnership	100	
B Britten Ltd	80	
		240
		765
Less: outstanding lodgements	220	
	300	
		520
Balance at bank as per bank statement		245

THE BANK STATEMENT

A bank statement is a copy of a bank account as shown by the bank records. Bank statements are sent out to customers on a regular basis, for example every month, or they can be viewed online. This enables the customer to check their funds in the bank (or borrowing on overdraft) regularly and to update their own records of transactions that have occurred. It could be, for example, that the bank has not previously notified them of a certain deduction from the account, for example bank charges.

An example of a bank statement is shown below: If you are not familiar with the details of payments – eg SO (standing order), DD (direct debit), BGC (bank giro credit), BACS (Bankers Automated Clearing Services) – see Chapter 4.

STATEMENT				National Bank PLC
				5-6 Christmas Square
				Mereford
				MR1 7GH

Account	Teme Computers
Account Number	12037661
Sheet	17
Date	31 October 2011

Date	Details	Debit	Credit	Balance	
2011					
01 Oct	Balance			405.93	CR
03 Oct	Cheques		590.53	996.46	CR
07 Oct	619651	298.64		697.82	CR
07 Oct	619652	100.00		597.82	CR
13 Oct	RT Telecom (DD)	154.00		443.82	CR
14 Oct	619653	58.90		384.92	CR
17 Oct	Mereford City Council (SO)	240.00		144.92	CR
21 Oct	GH Trading (BGC)		230.00	374.92	CR
21 Oct	Cheque		127.80	502.72	CR
24 Oct	Cash		450.00	952.72	CR
24 Oct	Tombenco (BACS)		120.50	1073.22	CR
27 Oct	Iveco (DD)	127.80		945.42	CR
31 Oct	619654	45.75		899.67	CR
31 Oct	Bank charges	24.30		875.37	CR

WHY DO YOU NEED A BANK RECONCILIATION STATEMENT?

reconciliation

'Reconciliation' between the cash book and the bank statement final balance simply means **an explanation of the differences**. This explanation takes the form of a calculation (see page 183 for an example). The process can be seen as follows:

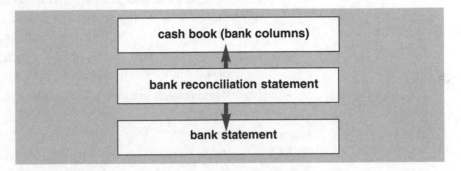

Differences between the cash book and the bank statement can arise from:

- **timing** of the recording of the transactions
- **errors** made by the business, or by the bank

We will explain each of these in turn.

timing differences – items recorded in the cash book

When a business compares the balance according to its cash book with the balance as shown by the bank statement there is often a difference. This difference can be caused by the **timing** of payments. For example:

- A cashier may send cheques out to suppliers, some of whom may pay in the cheque at the bank immediately while others may keep the cheque for several days before paying it in. When this happens the cashier will have recorded all the payments in the cash book. However, the bank records will only show the cheques that have actually been paid in by the suppliers and deducted from the business bank account.

  These cheques are known as **unpresented cheques**.

- With another type of timing difference – known as **outstanding lodgements** – the firm's cashier records a receipt in the cash book as he or she prepares the bank paying-in slip. However, the receipt may not be recorded by the bank on the bank statement on the same day, particularly if it is paid in late in the day, or if it is paid in at a bank branch other than the one at which the account is maintained.

timing differences – items not recorded in the cash book

payments in

Another timing difference may also occur when the bank has received a direct payment from a customer of the business. In this instance the bank's computer will have recorded the receipt in the business's account at the bank but the business may not be aware of the payment and will not, therefore, have recorded the receipt in the cash book. This type of payment includes:

– standing orders and BACS direct credits, ie incoming BACS payments received on the account, eg payments from customers when the payment has not been advised to the business

– bank giro credit amounts received by the bank, eg payments from customers when the payment has not been advised

– interest and refunds credited by the bank

payments out

Another reason why the balance of the cash book and the balance of the bank statement may not agree is because the bank may have deducted items from the customer's account, but the customer may not be aware of the deduction until the bank statement arrives. Examples of these deductions include:

– standing order and direct debit payments which the customer did not know about

– bank charges for running the account

– interest charged for overdrawn balances

differences caused by errors

Sometimes the difference between the two balances may be accounted for by an error on the part of the bank or an error in the cash book of the business. It is for this reason that a bank reconciliation is carried out frequently so that errors may be identified and rectified as soon as possible.

It is good business practice to prepare a bank reconciliation statement each time a bank statement is received. The reconciliation statement should be prepared as quickly as possible so that any queries – either with the bank statement or in the firm's cash book – can be resolved. Many firms will specify to their accounting staff the timescales for preparing bank reconciliation statements. For example, if the bank statement is received weekly, then the reconciliation statement should be prepared within five working days.

PREPARING THE BANK RECONCILIATION STATEMENT

When a bank statement has been received, reconciliation of the two balances is carried out in the following way:

step 1   The cashier will tick off the items that appear in both the cash book and the bank statement.

step 2   The unticked items on the bank statement are entered into the bank columns of the cash book to bring it up to date.

step 3   The bank columns of the cash book are now balanced to find the revised figure.

step 4   The remaining unticked items from the cash book will be the timing differences.

step 5   The timing differences are used to prepare the bank reconciliation statement (see below).

We will explain how this procedure is carried out in the Case Study which follows on the next page. First, however, we will revise what we have covered in this chapter so far by looking at a specimen bank reconciliation statement. Study the format shown below and the explanatory notes. Relate them to the text on the previous two pages.

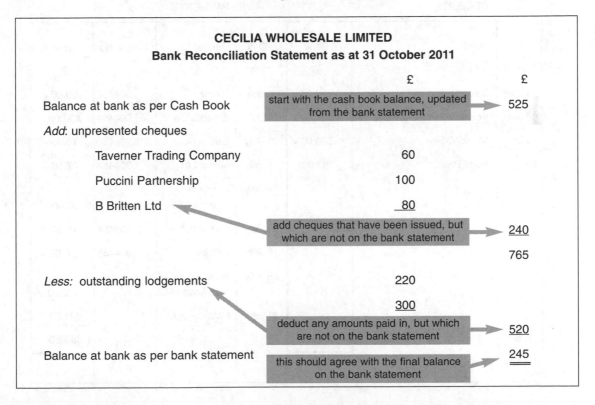

CECILIA WHOLESALE LIMITED
Bank Reconciliation Statement as at 31 October 2011

	£	£
Balance at bank as per Cash Book	*start with the cash book balance, updated from the bank statement*	525
Add: unpresented cheques		
Taverner Trading Company	60	
Puccini Partnership	100	
B Britten Ltd	80	
	add cheques that have been issued, but which are not on the bank statement	240
		765
Less: outstanding lodgements	220	
	300	
	deduct any amounts paid in, but which are not on the bank statement	520
Balance at bank as per bank statement	*this should agree with the final balance on the bank statement*	245

Case study

HURST & CO: BANK RECONCILIATION STATEMENT

situation

Carol works as a cashier for Hurst & Co., Solicitors. Her responsibilities include entering and maintaining the firm's cash book and preparing a bank reconciliation statement at the end of the month.

The firm's cash book for July 2011 which Carol has just finished entering and balancing for the month end is shown below (Note: for the sake of clarity the cash column has been omitted.) A copy of the firm's bank statement from the Star Bank Limited dated 31 July 2011 has just been received and is also illustrated on the next page. The numerical difference between the two is:

Bank statement £903.00 *minus* cash book £641.70 = £261.30

This is the difference which Carol will have to 'reconcile'.

Carol now follows the five steps outlined on the previous page.

Step 1 – tick off the items in both cash book and bank statement

Carol ticks off the items that appear in both the cash book and the bank statement.

Hurst & Co – Cash Book

	RECEIPTS				PAYMENTS		
Date	Details	Bank		Date	Details	Cheque No.	Bank
2011		£		2011			£
1 July	Balance b/d	756.20 ✓		1 July	T Able	004450	50.00 ✓
4 July	Kershaw Ltd	220.00 ✓		1 July	Broad & Co	004451	130.00
15 July	Morris & Son	330.00 ✓		1 July	Gee & Co	004452	10.00 ✓
29 July	Potts Bros	63.00		8 July	Minter Ltd	004453	27.50
				14 July	Liverport City Council (DD)		89.00 ✓
				14 July	F D Jewell	004454	49.00 ✓
				15 July	Kirk Ltd	004455	250.00 ✓
				26 July	Bond Insurance (SO)		122.00 ✓
				31 July	Balance c/d		641.70
		1,369.20					1,369.20
31 July	Balance b/d	641.70					

STATEMENT

Star Bank PLC
23 Market Street
Liverport
LP1 6TG

Account	Hurst & Co
Account Number	79014456
Sheet	17
Date	31 July 2011

Date	Details	Debit	Credit	Balance	
2011					
01 July	Balance			756.20	Cr ✓
05 July	Cheques		220.00 ✓	976.20	Cr
08 July	004450	50.00 ✓		926.20	Cr
14 July	004452	10.00 ✓		916.20	Cr
15 July	Liverport City Council (DD)	89.00 ✓		827.20	Cr
19 July	Cheques		330.00 ✓	1,157.20	Cr
25 July	004455	250.00 ✓		907.20	Cr
26 July	Bond Insurance (SO)	122.00 ✓		785.20	Cr
29 July	004454	49.00 ✓		736.20	Cr
29 July	Bank charges	12.95		723.25	Cr
29 July	Ricardo Limited (BGC)		179.75	903.00	Cr

step 2 – update the cash book from the bank statement

The unticked items on the bank statement indicate items that have gone through the bank account but have not yet been entered in Hurst & Co's cash book. These are:

| Receipt | 29 July | BGC, Ricardo Limited | £179.75 |
| Payment | 29 July | Bank Charges | £12.95 |

Carol will now need to enter these items in the cash book to bring it up to date (see next page). The new entries are shown in darker type, the previous entries are in lighter type.

step 3 – balance the cash book bank columns to produce an updated balance

Carol now balances the bank columns of the cash book off again, as shown on the next page.

The balance of the bank column now stands at £808.50. This still differs from the bank statement balance of £903.00.

Hurst & Co – Cash Book (extract)

RECEIPTS			PAYMENTS			
Date 2011	Details	Bank £	Date 2011	Details	Cheque number	Bank £
			31 July	Balance c/d		641.70
		1,369.20				1,369.20
31 July	Balance b/d	641.70	29 July	Bank Charges		12.95
29 July	Ricardo Limited (BGC)	179.75	31 July	Balance c/d		808.50
		821.45				821.45
1 Aug	Balance b/d	808.50				

The numerical difference between the two is:

Bank statement £903.00 *minus* cash book £808.50 = £94.50

This remaining difference is dealt with in the bank reconciliation statement.

step 4 – identify the remaining unticked items from the cash book

There are some items that remain unticked in the cash book. These are:

Receipt	29 July	Potts Bros	£63.00
Payments	1 July	Broad & Co (cheque no. 004451)	£130.00
	8 July	Minter Ltd (cheque no. 004453)	£ 27.50

These items should appear on next month's bank statement and are timing differences. These are the items which will be required in the preparation of the bank reconciliation statement, which is Carol's next step.

step 5 – preparation of the bank reconciliation statement

The completed statement is shown on the next page. The stages followed in its completion are as follows:

1   **enter the cash book balance**

The balance figure to use, as 'per the cash book', is the revised cash book balance after entering the items that appeared on the bank statement which had not previously been entered, ie £808.50.

2   add unpresented cheques

The unpresented cheques are the cheques that Hurst & Co has issued, but which have not yet been deducted from the firm's bank account, probably because they have not yet been paid in by the suppliers. They are:

Broad & Co (cheque no. 004451)	£130.00
Minter Ltd (cheque no. 004453)	£ 27.50
Total	£157.50

The unpresented cheques totalling £157.50 are added to the cash book balance in the bank reconciliation statement, bringing the revised cash book balance to £966.00. They are added back to the cash book balance so that both the cash book and the bank account contain the same items.

3   deduct outstanding bank lodgement

A 'bank lodgement' represents money, ie cheques and/or cash, that has been received by a business, entered into the cash book and paid into the bank. In this case, however, the deposit has been made too late to appear on the firm's bank statement, and so forms part of the difference, as an 'outstanding' lodgement.

Here the bank lodgement of £63.00 is deducted in the bank reconciliation statement from the subtotal of £966.00, ie £966.00 − £63.00 = £903.00.

4   completing the reconciliation

Now that all the outstanding items have been added or deducted, the recalculated balance on the bank reconciliation statement should be the same as the final bank statement balance. A comparison of the two shows that they are both £903.00. Carol has successfully completed the reconciliation.

HURST & CO **Bank Reconciliation Statement as at 31 July 2011**		
	£	£
Balance at bank as per Cash Book		808.50
Add: unpresented cheques		
Broad & Co	130.00	
Minter Ltd	27.50	
		157.50
		966.00
Less: outstanding lodgement		63.00
Balance at bank as per bank statement		903.00

DEALING WITH OVERDRAFTS

positive bank balances

In the Case Study and examples so far in this chapter we have dealt with bank reconciliation statements where the bank balance has been positive – ie there has been money in the bank account. We have also dealt with cash books which have shown that there there is money in the bank.

A positive bank balance has been indicated by:

- in the **cash book** – a debit (left-hand) brought down balance
- a **bank statement** where the balance is followed by 'CR' – which stands for 'credit' and to the bank and the customer means that there is money in the account

negative bank balances

Businesses sometimes have overdrafts at the bank. Overdrafts are where the bank account becomes negative and the business in effect borrows from the bank. This is shown:

- in the **cash book** as a credit (right-hand) brought down balance
- on the **bank statement** where the balance is followed by 'DR' (or sometimes by 'OD') – which to the bank and the customer means that there is an overdraft

reconciliation statements and overdrafts

If you want to show an overdraft on a bank reconciliation statement, you should treat it as a negative figure by placing it in brackets. As far as the calculation is concerned, it is simply a matter of using the minus key on the calculator. If in the Case Study earlier in this chapter, Hurst & Co had started the month with an overdraft of £808.50 (a credit balance in the cash book), you would key the following into the calculator (the black boxes represent the calculator keys):

–	£808.50
+	£157.50
–	£63
=	*produces a total of (£714.00)*

Now look at how the bank reconciliation statement is set out on the next page, using brackets for negative figures (ie overdrafts).

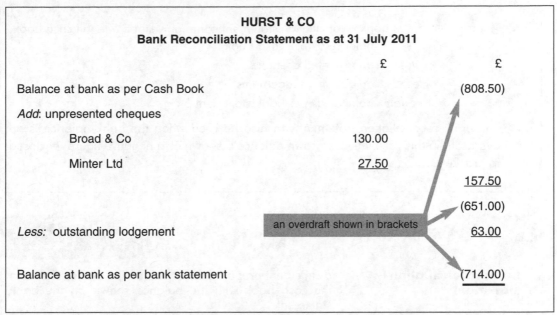

HURST & CO
Bank Reconciliation Statement as at 31 July 2011

	£	£
Balance at bank as per Cash Book		(808.50)
Add: unpresented cheques		
Broad & Co	130.00	
Minter Ltd	27.50	
		157.50
		(651.00)
Less: outstanding lodgement	an overdraft shown in brackets	63.00
Balance at bank as per bank statement		(714.00)

a bank reconciliation statement starting and ending with an overdraft

Chapter summary

- The balance of the bank account in the cash book of a business is regularly compared with the balance on the bank statement to ensure that the accounting records of both the business and the bank contain the same transactions and that no errors have occurred.

- There are inevitably differences between the cash book balance and the bank statement balance. These are caused either by errors in the cash book or bank statement, or by timing differences between the two documents.

- Timing differences may arise from items recorded in the bank statement and not in the cash book, bank charges and bank giro credits, for example. Normally the cash book is updated when these items are identified on the bank statement.

- Other timing differences might arise from items recorded in the cash book and not on the bank statement, unpresented cheques and outstanding lodgements, for example.

- These items are recorded in a bank reconciliation statement which is a calculation explaining how the unpresented cheques and outstanding lodgements are causing the difference between the cash book and the bank statement balances.

(continued on next page)

- The formula of the bank reconciliation statement commonly starts with the cash book:

  balance as per cash book

  plus   unpresented cheques

  less   outstanding lodgements

  equals   balance as per bank statement

- The bank reconciliation statement can also be used when the bank balance is an overdraft. In this case, the overdrawn balance is shown as a negative figure, enclosed in brackets.

Key terms

bank reconciliation statement	a statement prepared to link the bank balance shown in the cash book with the balance shown on the bank statement
timing differences	discrepancies between the bank statement and the cash book that will be corrected over time, such as unpresented cheques and outstanding lodgements
outstanding lodgements	amounts that have been paid into the bank, but not yet recorded on the bank statement
unpresented cheques	cheques that have been issued but have not yet been paid in and deducted from the account of the business

Exercises

Answers to the asterisked questions are to be found at the back of this book.

A blank bank reconciliation statement is reproduced on the next page and the format for setting out the cash book is shown below. You may photocopy and adapt these formats.

These forms are also reproduced at the end of this book and are available for download from the Resources section of www.osbornebooks.co.uk

CASH BOOK						
RECEIPTS			PAYMENTS			
Date	Details	Bank	Date	Details	Cheque no.	Bank
2011		£	2011			£

**name of
business**..

Bank Reconciliation Statement as at ....

	£	£
Balance at bank as per Cash Book		-------------------------
Add: unpresented cheque(s)		

Less: outstanding lodgement(s)		

Balance at bank as per bank statement		-------------------------

Note
Negative bank balances (ie overdrafts) should be shown in brackets.

8.1* You are a trainee accountant for Fern Limited, a small printing company. One of your tasks is to enter transactions in the company's cash book, check the entries on receipt of the bank statement, update the cash book and make any amendments as necessary. You are then asked to prepare a bank reconciliation statement at the end of the month.

The company's cash book (showing the bank money columns only) and the bank statement are shown below.

You are to:

- Reconcile the cash book with the bank statement.

- Make the entries necessary to update the cash book.

- Balance the bank columns of the cash book and calculate the revised bank balance.

- Draw up or obtain a copy of a blank bank reconciliation statement.

- Start with the balance as per the cash book, list any unpresented cheques and sub-total on the reconciliation statement.

- Enter details of bank lodgements.

- Calculate the balance as per the bank statement and check your total against the bank statement for accuracy.

Fern Ltd – Cash Book

CASH BOOK

	RECEIPTS				PAYMENTS		
Date	Details	Bank	Date	Details	Cheque no.	Bank
2011		£	2011			£
1 Aug	Balance b/d	1,946	2 Aug	DD Bell Insurance		75
1 Aug	I Watts & Co	249	2 Aug	Harvey & Co	200100	206
5 Aug	B Rogers (BACS)	188	4 Aug	Durose Ltd	200101	315
8 Aug	E Shaw	150	8 Aug	Motts Garage	200102	211
10 Aug	J Moore Ltd	440	9 Aug	SO Rock Finance		120
18 Aug	Simms Ltd	65	12 Aug	Hill Bros	200103	22
26 Aug	Martin Black	520	22 Aug	Ashleys Ltd	200104	137
30 Aug	Davies Partners	82	26 Aug	DD Rates		270
			31 Aug	Balance c/d		2,284
		3,640				3,640
31 Aug	Balance b/d	2,284				

ALBION BANK   **STATEMENT**

12 Market Street, Bury BU1 2GH

Account   Fern Limited   **Account no.**   78300582

Date   31 August 2011   **Statement No.**   16

Date	Details	Debit	Credit	Balance	
2011					
1 Aug	Balance			1,946	CR
2 Aug	Cheques		249	2,195	CR
4 Aug	Bell Insurance (DD)	75		2,120	CR
4 Aug	200101	315		1,805	CR
5 Aug	B Rogers (BACS)		188	1,993	CR
8 Aug	Cheques		150	2,143	CR
10 Aug	200102	211		1,932	CR
12 Aug	Cheques		440	2,372	CR
12 Aug	Rock Finance (SO)	120		2,252	CR
20 Aug	Cheques		65	2,317	CR
26 Aug	DD Rates	270		2,047	CR
30 Aug	Torr Bros (BGC)		92	2,139	CR
31 Aug	Bank Charges	55		2,084	CR
31 Aug	City Finance (SO)	1,000		1,084	CR

8.2* You are employed by Brooklyn Ltd as their cashier. Your main responsibility is to maintain the company's cash book and prepare a bank reconciliation statement at the end of each month.

The cash book (showing the bank money columns only) is set out below together with a copy of the bank statement for February 2011.

You are to:

- Reconcile the cash book with the bank statement.

- Make the entries necessary to update the cash book.

- Balance the bank columns of the cash book and calculate the revised bank balance.

- Draw up or obtain a copy of a blank bank reconciliation statement.

- Start with the balance as per the cash book, list any unpresented cheques and sub-total on the reconciliation statement.

- Enter details of bank lodgements.

- Calculate the balance as per the bank statement and check your total against the bank statement for accuracy.

Brooklyn Ltd – Cash Book

CASH BOOK

	RECEIPTS			PAYMENTS		
Date	Details	Bank	Date	Details	Cheque no.	Bank
2011			2011			
1 Feb	Balance b/d	1,425	1 Feb	Barton Bros	400460	98
1 Feb	Worrall & Co	157	1 Feb	Road Car Co (SO)		50
4 Feb	Brindle's (BGC)	243	3 Feb	R Jackson Ltd	400461	540
8 Feb	Robinson Ltd	91	9 Feb	Spencer Partners	400462	42
14 Feb	Moore & Cox (BGC)	75	9 Feb	Avery Computers	400463	490
21 Feb	Riley & Co	420	10 Feb	Ajax Insurance (DD)		300
28 Feb	Howard Ltd	94	16 Feb	Shanklin Garage	400464	110
			23 Feb	Petty Cash	400465	50
			28 Feb	White & Co	400466	120
			28 Feb	Balance c/d		705
		2,505				2,505
28 Feb	Balance b/d	705				

REGENCY BANK			STATEMENT		
10 The Parade, Cheltenham G12 6YG					
Account Brooklyn Limited			**Account no.** 29842943		
Date 28 February 2011			**Statement No.** 35		

Date 2011	Details	Debit	Credit	Balance	
1 Feb	Balance			1,425	CR
2 Feb	Cheques		157	1,582	CR
2 Feb	Road Car Co (SO)	50		1,532	CR
4 Feb	400460	98		1,434	CR
6 Feb	Brindle's (BGC)		243	1,677	CR
10 Feb	Cheques		91	1,768	CR
12 Feb	Ajax Insurance (DD)	300		1,468	CR
14 Feb	Moore & Cox (BGC)		75	1,543	CR
14 Feb	400463	490		1,053	CR
23 Feb	Cheques		420	1,473	CR
26 Feb	Rates (DD)	103		1,370	CR
26 Feb	400465	50		1,320	CR
27 Feb	D Stead (BACS)		220	1,540	CR
28 Feb	Bank Charges	38		1,502	CR

8.3*   As accounts assistant for O'Connor Limited your main task is to enter transactions into the company's cash book, check the entries against the bank statement and prepare a monthly bank reconciliation statement.

The cash book (showing the bank money columns only) and bank statement for October 2011 are set out below.

You are to:

*   Reconcile the cash book with the bank statement.

*   Make the entries necessary to update the cash book.

*   Balance the bank columns of the cash book and calculate the revised bank balance.

*   Draw up or obtain a copy of a blank bank reconciliation statement.

*   Start with the balance as per the cash book, list any unpresented cheques and sub-total on the reconciliation statement.

*   Enter details of bank lodgements.

*   Calculate the balance as per the bank statement and check your total against the bank statement for accuracy.

<table>
<tr><td colspan="8" align="center">**O'Connor Limited – Cash Book**
CASH BOOK</td></tr>
<tr><td colspan="3" align="center">RECEIPTS</td><td colspan="5" align="center">PAYMENTS</td></tr>
<tr><td>Date</td><td>Details</td><td>Bank</td><td>Date</td><td>Details</td><td>Cheque no.</td><td>Bank</td></tr>
<tr><td>2011</td><td></td><td></td><td>2011</td><td></td><td></td><td></td></tr>
<tr><td>1 Oct</td><td>Balance b/d</td><td>2,521</td><td>1 Oct</td><td>Sharp & Co Rent (SO)</td><td></td><td>400</td></tr>
<tr><td>4 Oct</td><td>Allen Ltd (BACS)</td><td>620</td><td>4 Oct</td><td>G Orwell</td><td>210526</td><td>367</td></tr>
<tr><td>7 Oct</td><td>Mason & Moore</td><td>27</td><td>5 Oct</td><td>Heath & Co</td><td>210527</td><td>1,108</td></tr>
<tr><td>11 Oct</td><td>Howard Limited</td><td>48</td><td>7 Oct</td><td>Ellis & Son</td><td>210528</td><td>320</td></tr>
<tr><td>11 Oct</td><td>Barrett & Bryson</td><td>106</td><td>13 Oct</td><td>Kerr's Garage</td><td>210529</td><td>32</td></tr>
<tr><td>12 Oct</td><td>D Patel (BGC)</td><td>301</td><td>14 Oct</td><td>J Choudrey</td><td>210530</td><td>28</td></tr>
<tr><td>20 Oct</td><td>Cohen & Co</td><td>58</td><td>21 Oct</td><td>Astley Insurance (DD)</td><td></td><td>139</td></tr>
<tr><td>25 Oct</td><td>J McGilvery</td><td>209</td><td>25 Oct</td><td>Text Computers</td><td>210531</td><td>1,800</td></tr>
<tr><td>31 Oct</td><td>Balance c/d</td><td>604</td><td>30 Oct</td><td>Rates (DD)</td><td></td><td>300</td></tr>
<tr><td></td><td></td><td>4,494</td><td></td><td></td><td></td><td>4,494</td></tr>
<tr><td></td><td></td><td></td><td>1 Nov</td><td>Balance b/d</td><td></td><td>604</td></tr>
</table>

OAK BANK   STATEMENT

99 Bank Chambers, Nottingham NG1 7FG

Account   O'Connor Limited   **Account no.**   06618432

Date   31 October 2011   **Statement No.** 45

Date 2011	Details	Debit	Credit	Balance	
1Oct	Balance			2,521	CR
1 Oct	Sharp & Co (SO)	400		2,121	CR
4 Oct	Allen Ltd (BACS)		620	2,741	CR
7 Oct	210526	367		2,374	CR
11 Oct	Cheques		154	2,528	CR
13 Oct	D Patel (BGC)		301	2,829	CR
15 Oct	Cheques		27	2,856	CR
18 Oct	210528	320		2,536	CR
18 Oct	210527	1,108		1,428	CR
21 Oct	Astley Insurance (DD)	139		1,289	CR
27 Oct	210531	1,800		511	DR
28 Oct	Bayley's (BACS)		114	397	DR
29 Oct	Rates (DD)	300		697	DR
29 Oct	Bank Interest	53		750	DR
29 Oct	Bank Charges	45		795	DR

8.4 You are the cashier of Chowda Trading Limited and have written up the firm's cash book (bank money columns only) for the month of September 2011. You have also received the bank statement for the same period.

You are to:

- Reconcile the cash book with the bank statement.

- Make the entries necessary to update the cash book.

- Balance the bank columns of the cash book and calculate the revised bank balance.

- Draw up or obtain a copy of a blank bank reconciliation statement.

- Start with the balance as per the cash book, list any unpresented cheques and sub-total on the reconciliation statement.

- Enter details of bank lodgements.

- Calculate the balance as per the bank statement and check your total against the bank statement for accuracy.

Chowda Trading Limited – Cash Book						
CASH BOOK						
RECEIPTS				PAYMENTS		
Date	Details	Bank	Date	Details	Cheque no.	Bank
2011			2011			
1 Sept	Rogers & Co	2,710	1 Sept	Balance b/d		4,223
6 Sept	Chapman Ltd	252	6 Sept	Park Lane Garage	043173	236
8 Sept	F Sanderson (BACS)	121	6 Sept	Wages	043174	1,723
9 Sept	Booth (BACS)	379	7 Sept	Otis Electronics	043175	110
16 Sept	Rushton Associates	1,200	12 Sept	Fraser & Co	043176	46
20 Sept	I Campbell	28	18 Sept	United Insurance (DD)		175
27 Sept	W Blake (BGC)	1,320	23 Sept	Beet & Malkin	043177	1,052
28 Sept	Chapman Ltd	540	26 Sept	Rates (SO)		220
28 Sept	Balance c/d	1,235				
		7,785				7,785
			1 Oct	Balance b/d		1,235

STAR BANK

STATEMENT

16, South Parade, Offerton OF1 8BN

Account   Chowda Trading Limited

Account no.   77650017

Date   30 September 2011

Statement No.   16

Date 2011	Details	Debit	Credit	Balance	
1 Sept	Balance			4,223	DR
6 Sept	043174	1,723		5,946	DR
6 Sept	043173	236		6,182	DR
7 Sept	Cheque		2,710	3,472	DR
7 Sept	Cheque		252	3,220	DR
9 Sept	Sanderson (BACS)		121	3,099	DR
13 Sept	Booth (BACS)		379	2,720	DR
14 Sept	Bank Charges	20		2,740	DR
14 Sept	Bank Interest	92		2,832	DR
18 Sept	Cheque		1,200	1,632	DR
18 Sept	United Insurance (DD)	175		1,807	DR
18 Sept	0043176	46		1,853	DR
23 Sept	Cheque		28	1,825	DR
28 Sept	W Blake (BGC)		1,320	505	DR
28 Sept	Rates (SO)	220		725	DR
28 Sept	Hunt & Associates (BACS)		26	699	DR

9 Principles of petty cash

what this chapter covers . . .

This chapter:

- explains the principles of maintaining a petty cash system using the imprest system

- shows the completion of the petty cash vouchers for expenses

- describes the importance of checking details on the vouchers, including amounts claimed

- covers the authorisation of vouchers including signatures

- explains the principles and procedures of VAT

- explains the importance of accuracy

- explains the importance of keeping the petty cash safe and secure

OCR assessment criteria covered

Unit M5: Maintaining petty cash records

1.1 Prepare petty cash vouchers

1.2 Calculate the purchase tax (eg VAT) where the expense includes it

INTRODUCTION TO PETTY CASH

All businesses and organisations regularly incur small items of expenditure. Often these expenses are paid for by cash since the amount required may be too small for the payment to be made by cheque. Such examples of this type of expense could be payment of postage stamps, travelling expenses, small items of stationery, and so on. Such small items of expenses are usually recorded in the petty cash book that is designed specifically for this purpose. Other expenditure incurring larger amounts of money is recorded in the cash book and this is dealt with in Unit M3 (Chapters 6-7).

THE PETTY CASH PROCEDURE

The business will appoint a petty cashier, often a junior member of staff, who is responsible for looking after the petty cash on behalf of the main cashier. The main cashier will provide the petty cashier with a sum of money, called a 'float'. The petty cashier is then responsible for this money, making payments to members of staff to repay them for expenses incurred on behalf of the business and keeping records of payments made, amounts received and balancing the petty cash book at regular intervals.

The petty cashier will need the following to carry out this task:

* a petty cash book in which to record transactions
* a lockable petty cash box to hold the money
* a stock of blank petty cash vouchers (see page 204) for claims on petty cash to be made
* a secure place (eg a lockable drawer) in which to keep these items

making a claim

Before studying the form-filling procedures we will look at how a claim for petty cash is made by an employee with the following example:

John works for Harpers Estate Agents as an office junior. His supervisor, Mrs May, asks John to go to the post office and buy postage stamps for the office. John carries out this request as follows:

* John goes to the post office and buys the postage stamps for the office. He pays £4.20 for them in cash and asks for a receipt.
* On his return to the office John gives the stamps and receipt to Mrs May.
* Mrs May authorises a petty cash voucher that details the purchase of the postage stamps made by John and attaches the receipt to the voucher.

- The petty cashier gives John £4.20 in cash.
- The petty cashier enters the details in the petty cash book.

items claimed for by petty cash

As already mentioned, petty cash is used to make small cash payments for purchases and expenses incurred by the business. Examples of the type of payments made from petty cash include:

- postage
- small items of stationery
- casual labour
- window cleaning
- travel expenses such as bus and rail fares incurred on behalf of the business
- donations

Note, however, that petty cash should not be used to pay for private expenses of employees, eg tea, coffee and milk, unless the business has agreed these in advance. Usually there will be a list of approved expenses that can be reimbursed from petty cash.

The business will also decide on the maximum value for any transaction that can be paid out of petty cash; for example, £25 is a common figure.

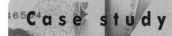

Case study

PETTY CASH EXPENSES

situation

You are employed as an accounts assistant for Astley Controls Limited. One of your duties is that of petty cashier. Which of the following expenses would you allow to be paid out of the petty cash? The upper limit for petty cash transactions is £25.

- Postage stamps, £6.50
- Window cleaning, £8.00
- Envelopes for office use, £3.20
- Computer disks, £38.50
- Coffee and milk for the office, £5.76
- Donation to a local charity, £10.00
- Train fare to work £4.60 claimed by the office assistant
- Car mileage to work of Manager who was called in on Sunday morning following a break-in of the premises

solution

Postage	pay from petty cash
Window cleaning	pay from petty cash
Envelopes	pay from petty cash
Computer disks	this is a business expense but, since the amount is £38.50 it is too large to be paid out of petty cash, instead it should be paid by cheque
Coffee and milk	this payment can only be made out of petty cash if the items were used for the use of official visitors and customers and not for use by the employees
Donation	pay from petty cash
Train fare	this is a personal expense and cannot be paid for out of petty cash
Car mileage	travel to work is a personal expense, as seen from the previous item; however, as this expense was a special journey on a Sunday following a break-in to the premises, it can be paid from petty cash

Notes on the case study

• If the petty cashier cannot decide whether or not an item of expense can be paid from petty cash, the item should be referred to the accounts supervisor for a decision.

• Before payments can be made for petty cash expenses they must be supported by documentary evidence and be properly authorised (see below).

THE IMPREST SYSTEM

As mentioned above, the petty cashier is given a 'float' of money at the beginning of the period to enable payments to be made for expenses incurred during the period. At the end of the period the amount spent is added up, this amount is then reclaimed from the cashier to restore the money to the original float. It is the same principle as filling up the tank of your car each week. The amount of fuel you put in is the same as the amount you have used. The following example illustrates the procedure:

		£
January 1	Float received from cashier	100.00
January 31	Amount spent during month	70.00
	Balance of cash in hand	30.00
February 1	Amount received from cashier to restore float to original amount	70.00
	Cash at start of next month ie imprest	100.00

If, during the period, all the cash is used up then it is possible to obtain further amounts of money from the cashier to top up the float. It is also possible to increase the float from time to time if extra money is required for additional expenditure .

advantages of using the imprest system

One advantage of using the imprest system is that it is possible to check the cash at any time since the total of expenditure incurred during a period together with the cash in hand should always equal the original float. Another advantage is that small items of expenditure can be recorded separately in the petty cash book thereby eliminating such items from the main cash book. Since this task can be carried out by a junior member of staff it saves the cashier valuable time that can then be spent in other areas of work.

PETTY CASH VOUCHER

When an employee incurs expenditure on behalf of the business and then wishes to get the money back he/she will have to complete a petty cash voucher and provide documentary evidence such as a receipt if possible. Petty cash vouchers contain the following details:

- details of expenditure together with a receipt for money spent (if possible)
- amount spent, including VAT, if applicable
- signature of person making the claim and to whom the money will be paid
- signature of person authorising the payment, usually the petty cashier for amounts within the authorisation limit, larger amounts will be authorised by the accounts supervisor or manager
- the petty cash voucher will then be numbered to enable the documentation to be filed correctly and easily identified in the petty cash book

An example of a petty cash voucher is shown below.

petty cash voucher		No. 83
	date	6 December 2011

description		amount
	£	p
Train fare (no VAT)	5	83
	5	83

signature   *S J Worrall*

authorised   *J K Blake*

authorisation of petty cash vouchers

When the petty cashier receives a completed petty cash voucher from a member of staff it is important to check that the voucher has been completed correctly, signed by the person making the claim and has been properly authorised. It is important to check that the amount claimed for is within the authorised limit. For example, the organisation may allow payments to be made by petty cash up to £25 as already mentioned above. The petty cashier should also check the voucher for accuracy in the calculations and wherever possible ensure that a receipt is attached to the voucher.

The petty cash voucher details are then entered in the petty cash book and the voucher filed away in numerical order so that it may be easily located if necessary.

PETTY CASH BOOK

A petty cash book is shown on the next page. Note the analysis columns that enable the transaction to be recorded and analysed at the same time, according to the type of expenditure incurred. We will look in detail at the entries that are made in the petty cash book in the next chapter.

VALUE ADDED TAX (VAT)

Most of the goods and services we buy are subject to Value Added Tax (VAT) which is added to the cost of the goods and services at the standard rate. In the UK all businesses above a certain level of turnover (sales) have to be registered for VAT which is administered by HM Revenue & Customs.

As stated above, VAT is charged by a business on its sales and is ultimately paid by the last 'purchaser' of the goods or services and 'collected' by the business selling the goods and services and then paid to HM Revenue & Customs.

VAT Rates

There are three VAT rates presently set by the government:

1 **Standard Rate @ 20%** – this tax is added to most goods and services such as electrical and household goods, car servicing, meals in a restaurant.

2 **Reduced Rate @ 5%** – this rate applies to certain goods and services for example domestic fuel or power for heating and the installation of energy saving materials.

Petty Cash Book

Receipts £ p	Date	Details	Voucher Number	Total Payments £ p	VAT £ p	Postage £ p	Stationery £ p	Refresh-ments £ p	Travel £ p	Sundry Expenses £ p

3   **Zero Rate @ 0%** – some goods and services are zero rated, which means that VAT is charged at 0%. Such goods and services include most food purchased from the supermarket, children's clothes and shoes, books and periodicals.

exempt goods and services

However, not all expenses are subject to VAT. Supplies that are **exempt** include financial services and certain types of education.

VAT and petty cash

For a business to reclaim the VAT charged by a supplier, a receipt or invoice must be obtained for the business expense incurred. The document must contain the supplier's name, address and most importantly the VAT registration number. Such a receipt or invoice usually identifies the cost of the item purchased, together with the VAT charged to give a total amount, as shown below.

INVOICE
Business Products & Co
Unit 3 Wellington Industrial Estate
Burton-upon-Trent
BT1 7TS
Vat Registration No. 501 2764 72

to Kerr and Partners High Street Burton-upon-Trent BT1 6FG	**invoice no.** K 4621/03 **date** 18 August 2011 **order no.** 04/9848

quantity	description	cat. no.	unit price (£)	£
4 reams	A4 photocopier paper	PP639T	3.00	12.00
			VAT at 20%	2.40
				14.40
terms: net monthly				

To prepare a petty cash voucher from this invoice and enter the details in the petty cash book is straightforward because all the figures are available on the invoice:

- £2.40 will be entered in the VAT column of the petty cash book
- £12.00 will be entered in the appropriate expense column (probably the 'Stationery' column)
- £14.40, the total amount paid, will be entered in the total column

documents not showing VAT

Sometimes, however, receipts are issued showing the total amount paid but not the amount of VAT incurred. This is quite normal practice for smaller amounts. An example of a receipt that does not identify the amount of VAT separately is shown below:

RECEIPT

Logan Labels & Co., Dunwoody Lane, Derby, DA8 6HJ

Tel: 01332 280421

Vat Registration No. 488 2720 76

No.123

date 23 Sept 2011

received with thanks from   R Dudek

the sum of   seven pounds and twenty pence

for   1 pack adhesive labels

cheque	——
cash	7.20
discount	——
total	7.20

signature   J Murphy

---

calculating the VAT amount when it is not shown

In the above case it will be necessary to calculate the amount of VAT included in the total price of the adhesive labels of £7.20.

This can be calculated by formula as shown on the next page.

The formula, with VAT at 20% is:

price including VAT divided by 1.2 = price before VAT is added on . . .

in this case . . .

£7.20 divided by 1.2 = £6.00 = price before VAT is added on

the VAT content is therefore:

£7.20 less £6.00 = £1.20

using the VAT fraction

Another method of calculating the VAT content of a total price where the VAT is not shown is to use the VAT fraction. For 20% VAT this is $^1/6$. All you have to do is to divide the total including VAT at 20% by 6.

In the case of the receipt on the previous page, you just divide the total amount of £7.20 by 6 to produce a VAT total of £1.20.

entries in the petty cash book

Whichever method you use, the £1.20 will be entered in the VAT column in the petty cash book, £6.00 in the appropriate expense column, and the full £7.20 in the total payment column.

Note that when calculating VAT amounts, fractions of a penny are ignored, ie the tax is normally rounded down to a whole penny. For example, the 20% VAT content of a total of £14.38 is £2.396666666. This is rounded down to £2.39.

SECURITY

It is important that the petty cash book and the money are kept in a safe and secure place. Ideally the money should be kept in a lockable cash box. The petty cashier should keep the key to the petty cash box in a safe place with a duplicate key being kept by the main cashier or accountant. The box together with the petty cash book should ideally be kept in a fireproof safe or cabinet. Only the petty cashier or main cashier should be authorised to make payments of petty cash and they should obtain a signature from the person receiving the money.

As mentioned above, one of the advantages of using the imprest system is that it is easy to check the petty cash at any time. This enables checks to be made on the petty cashier at various intervals to ensure that he or she is honest and the money is secure.

Chapter summary

- The petty cash book is used to record small items of cash expenditure incurred by a business.

- The person responsible for maintaining the petty cash book is called the petty cashier, and he or she is responsible for security.

- Most businesses operate petty cash using the imprest system. Initially a cash 'float' of a fixed amount of money is given to the petty cashier for a specific time period. During the period payment is made against the correct documentation – usually a petty cash voucher – which must be signed and authorised for payment. At the end of the period, any cash paid out is restored to the same amount for the beginning of the next week or month. This is known as the 'imprest' system.

- The advantage of using the imprest system is the ability to check the cash at any time since the total amount spent together with the cash in hand should always equal the original float. It also minimises the number of entries made in the main cash book.

- Petty cash vouchers are entered in the petty cash book and are analysed according to the type of expenditure incurred.

- If VAT has been paid it is important to analyse the relevant amount separately in the VAT column. If VAT is not shown separately on a receipt or petty cash voucher it may be necessary to calculate this figure to enable the VAT to be recorded in the appropriate column.

- It is important that the money is kept in a lockable box and – together with the petty cash book – kept in a secure place.

Key terms

cash float	an amount of money given to the petty cashier at the beginning of a period to enable them to make payments
imprest system	where money held in the petty cash float is restored to the original amount for the beginning of the next period
petty cash book	a book used for recording small items of cash expenditure which are usually analysed as they are entered
petty cashier	person responsible for the petty cash system
petty cash voucher	the form used to claim amounts from petty cash, which must be properly completed, signed and authorised

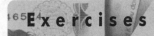

9.1 *   You are employed as petty cashier for a small advertising agency. The agency operates the petty cash imprest system in which small items of expenditure incurred by staff members up to £25.00 are paid by you, any item of expense above £25.00 is paid by cheque. The accountant asks you to look through a list of expenditure incurred by employees and to state which items should be paid by you out of petty cash, paid by the accountant by cheque and those items which you consider not to be business expenses.

(a)   Photo copier paper £12.60

(b)   Office cleaner £26.75

(c)   Postage on parcel to Hong Kong £3.74

(d)   Secretary's weekly train ticket to work £44.00

(e)   Tea, sugar and milk £4.92 for the office (given to visitors)

(f)   Coffee £5.20 for staff

(g)   Postage stamps £8.00

(h)   Card, fabric and staples for client's display £83.50

(i)   Advertisement in local press for new cleaner £21.70

(j)   Flowers for reception area £7.00

9.2 *   Morgan's Garage Limited employs several staff including James Dean, the accounts assistant, who unfortunately has to go into hospital for treatment and will be absent from work for the next four weeks. The garage operates their petty cash using the imprest system and one of James's tasks is that of petty cashier. James has a float of £200.00 that he uses to operate the imprest system on a monthly basis.

Whilst James is absent from work the owner of the garage, John Morgan, has asked Louise, the secretary, to look after the petty cash. To enable Louise to carry out this task John Morgan asks James to write some instructions on how the imprest system is used to operate the business's petty cash.

Task

Assume you are James and write brief notes on the operation of the petty cash using the imprest system. Ensure the instructions are clear and easy to follow.

9.3* As petty cashier you have been asked to prepare the petty cash vouchers, shown below, for signature by the person making the claim. You are to use today's date and are able to authorise payments up to £20.00; any amount above that is to be authorised by the cashier, Bob Allen. You are to assume that Bob Allen duly authorises any payment above £20.00. The next available petty cash voucher number is 22.

- Louise Carter purchased postage stamps totalling £18.30 (no VAT).

- Martin Gould purchased two computer memory sticks from Baxter's Stationers at a cost of £4.80 each, including VAT totalling £1.60.

- The office manager, Chris Edge, recently attended a training conference and wishes to be reimbursed for his train fare to London of £35.00 (no VAT).

State what other documentation would also be required besides the completed petty cash vouchers in each of the above.

Blank petty cash vouchers are reproduced on the pages that follow. You may photocopy them. Blank vouchers are also available at the end of the book and for download from the Resources section of www.osbornebooks.co.uk

petty cash voucher		No.
date		
description		amount
	£	p
signature		
authorised		

petty cash voucher		No.
date		
description		amount
	£	p
signature		
authorised		

petty cash voucher		No.
	date	
description		amount

	£	p

signature ....

authorised ....

9.4 Star Secretarial Agency has an office in Leeds and due to an increase in business has recently employed a new junior accounts assistant, Fred Grainger, who likes to be called Freddy. One of Freddy's duties is that of petty cashier and during Freddy's initial training he is shown the following instructions that must be followed when paying petty cash expenses to members of staff:

- All requests for payment of petty cash expenses must be made on petty cash vouchers showing full details of the expense, the date and if possible a receipt must be attached.

- Vouchers must be signed by the person claiming the money.

- Vouchers must be authorised for payment by the company secretary, Nick Burns.

- The petty cashier is authorised to pay claims up to £25.00, any item above that must be made by cheque.

- The agency uses the imprest system with a float of £100.00 for a two week period.

As petty cashier, Freddy, is asked to complete petty cash vouchers for any of the items shown below in accordance with the agency's instructions shown above.

STAR SECRETARIAL AGENCY

Details of transactions for 9 September 2011 are listed below. The last voucher used was No. 82.

- A4 copier paper for use in the office costing £15.60, including VAT of £2.60. This was bought by Joe Simpson, the assistant accountant, and a receipted invoice is attached.

- Nick Burns, the company secretary, gives you a receipt for the cost incurred in taking clients out for lunch, the bill totalled £57.60 including VAT of £9.60.

- Donation to the local church, £25.00, this was paid by Joe Simpson on behalf of the agency and a receipt obtained. No VAT.

- Postage stamps £9.00 paid for by Jane Adams the office administrator. No VAT.

- Train fare for employee, Alice Gee, to work £5.50. No VAT.

- Window cleaner £18.00 paid by Nick Burns, no receipt available. No VAT involved.

- Office milk, tea and coffee paid for by Jane Adams £12.30 (no VAT). The agency pays for these items for staff use.

Task

Assume you are Freddy. Complete, where appropriate, the petty cash vouchers. If, for any reason you are unable to pay a particular item you are to state why.

petty cash voucher			No.
date			
description		amount	
		£	p
signature			
authorised			

petty cash voucher			No.
date			
description		amount	
		£	p
signature			
authorised			

petty cash voucher   No.

date

description		amount
	£	p

signature ....

authorised ....

---

petty cash voucher   No.

date

description		amount
	£	p

signature ....

authorised ....

---

petty cash voucher   No.

date

description		amount
	£	p

signature ....

authorised ....

9.5* You are the petty cashier for Bode Manufacturers Ltd and have been given the following petty cash vouchers all of which include VAT at 20%. You have been asked to calculate the amount of VAT that will be shown in the VAT column of the petty cash book and the amount that will appear in the appropriate expense column.

Note that VAT amounts should always be rounded <u>down</u> to the nearest penny.

(a)	£21.60		(f)	£ 3.37
(b)	£ 2.40		(g)	92p
(c)	£ 8.58		(h)	£ 7.92
(d)	£ 1.44		(i)	£10.32
(e)	£16.32		(j)	£14.40

9.6 As petty cashier of The Holly Hotel you have been given the following petty cash vouchers, all of which include VAT at 20%. The hotel manager asks you to calculate the amount of VAT that will be shown in the VAT column of the petty cash book and the amount that will appear in the appropriate expense column.

Note that VAT amounts should always be rounded down (where appropriate) to the nearest penny.

(a)	£33.60	(f)	£7.20
(b)	·£25.92	(g)	£34.56
(c)	£1.92	(h)	£28.80
(d)	£4.80	(i)	96p
(e)	£ 5.76	(j)	£12.00

10 Writing up the petty cash book

what this chapter covers . . .

This chapter:

- shows the following entries into the petty cash book:
  - the opening balance brought down
  - the petty cash vouchers ensuring that the date, details of expenditure, amount and voucher number are entered correctly and into the appropriate expense analysis columns, accounting for any VAT paid

- illustrates how the petty cash book is totalled up at the end of the period with all columns accurately calculated and totalled

- explains how to cross cast the petty cash book

OCR assessment criteria covered

Unit M5: Maintaining petty cash records

2.1 List the petty cash vouchers into an analysed petty cash book ensuring that the expenses are entered and analysed

2.2 Account for any tax paid eg VAT

2.3 Total and cross cast the petty cash book

INTRODUCTION

As mentioned in the previous chapter, the petty cashier will be responsible for entering transactions into the petty cash book. Before entering the various transactions for the period the petty cashier will need to ensure that all the petty cash vouchers and receipts for transactions carried out during the period are available. They will also need the petty cash book and the cash box.

opening balance

The petty cash book will usually have an opening balance at the beginning of the period. The opening balance is the amount of money left over from the previous period, carried forward to the next week or month. This is illustrated in the following Case Study.

Case study

NEEDHAMS ADVERTISING AGENCY

situation

James Kerr is the petty cashier for Needhams Advertising Agency. The company operates their petty cash using the imprest system on a monthly period with a float of £100.00. At the end of May 2011 James entered the petty cash transactions and found he had spent £83.50 during May and had £16.50 left in his cash box.

As petty cashier James has been asked to carry out the following entries:

- enter the opening balance in the petty cash book at the beginning of June 2011
- enter the correct amount of cash, which has been collected from the bank to restore the imprest to £100.00.

solution

The opening balance for 1 June 2011 is £16.50, the amount of money left over from the last month. This figure needs to be brought forward to the start of the next period as follows:

Petty Cash Book (extract)

Receipts £ p	Date	Details	Voucher Number	Total Payments £ p
16.50	1 June	Balance b/d		

James now has to enter the amount of cash collected from the bank to restore the imprest. The amount needed to restore the imprest is as follows:

	£
Amount of float	100.00
Amount spent	83.50
Cash left over	16.50

Since £83.50 of the float has been spent as shown above the amount required to restore the imprest to £100.00 will be the amount spent £83.50. This can now be entered as follows:

Petty Cash Book (extract)

Receipts £ p	Date	Details	Voucher Number	Total Payments £ p
16.50	1 June	Balance b/d		
83.50	1 June	Cash		

entering transactions – payments

Most of the transactions recorded in the petty cash book relate to payments made by the petty cashier to members of staff to reimburse them for money spent on behalf of the business. Anyone incurring an expense on behalf of the business will have completed and signed a petty cash voucher that will also have been authorised by the petty cashier, manager or perhaps the accounts line manager.

It is important that the petty cashier ensures the petty cash vouchers have been properly completed and checks the calculations before entering them into the petty cash book.

The entry of petty cash vouchers into the petty cash book is shown in the Case Study 'Evans & Co' (see below).

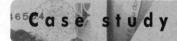

Case study

EVANS AND CO

situation

You are employed as accounts assistant for Evans & Co, and one of your responsibilities is that of petty cashier.

The company uses an analytical petty cash book, ie the petty cash book has columns which analyse the types of expenses. It also operates an imprest system.

There are a number of transactions for the week commencing 1 January 2011 that require entering in the petty cash book.

The next petty cash page to use is no. 2 in the book.

All transactions, unless otherwise stated, include VAT at 20%.

You are required to perform the following tasks:

1   Enter the opening balance into the petty cash book.

2   Enter the correct amount of cash that has been collected from the bank to restore the imprest to £100.

3   Enter the details of the petty cash vouchers that are shown below.

4   Total all the analysis columns and cross-check that the total agrees with the total payments column.

petty cash vouchers		
2011		£ p
1 Jan	Started the week with an opening balance	20.00
1 Jan	Received cash from bank to restore imprest	80.00
2 Jan	Paid for postage stamps (no VAT) on voucher no. 21	10.00
2 Jan	Paid for taxi fare for business use, voucher no. 22 (VAT of £1.60)	9.60
3 Jan	Paid for envelopes voucher no. 23 (VAT of £1.40)	8.40
4 Jan	Paid for registered package (no VAT) on voucher no. 24	12.50
5 Jan	Paid for office milk and tea (no VAT) voucher no. 25	6.24
6 Jan	Paid for postage stamps (no VAT) on voucher no. 26	10.00
6 Jan	Paid for suspension files voucher no. 27 (VAT of £2.16)	13.00
7 Jan	Paid for taxi fare to station voucher no. 28 (VAT of £1.00)	6.00

solution

The completed petty cash book appears as follows:

Petty Cash Book										PCB 2
Receipts £ p	Date	Details	Voucher Number	Total Payments £ p	VAT £ p	Postage £ p	Cleaning £ p	Travel £ p	Stationery £ p	Refresh- ments £ p
20.00	1 Jan	Balance b/d								
80.00	1 Jan	Cash								
	2 Jan	Postage stamps	21	10.00		10.00				
	2 Jan	Taxi fare	22	9.60	1.60			8.00		
	3 Jan	Envelopes	23	8.40	1.40				7.00	
	4 Jan	Registered package	24	12.50		12.50				
	5 Jan	Office milk and tea	25	6.24						6.24
	6 Jan	Postage stamps	26	10.00		10.00				
	6 Jan	Suspension files	27	13.00	2.17				10.84	
	7 Jan	Taxi fare	28	6.00	1.00			5.00		
				75.74	6.16	32.50		13.00	17.84	6.24

notes on completion of the petty cash book

- The receipts column is the 'debit side' of the petty cash book and contains the opening balance brought down of £20.00 plus the entry to record the money received from the bank to restore the imprest, in this case £80.00.

- Each item of expenditure is then entered as follows:

  (a) Enter the date. Note that it is important to ensure that the transactions are entered in strict date order. Then enter:

  - the exact details of the expenditure in the details column as they appear on the voucher
  - the voucher number in the voucher number column
  - the total amount spent on each transaction in the total payments column

  The total payment column is the 'credit side' of the petty cash book.

  (b) Using the analysis columns enter the amount of VAT, if applicable, in the VAT column and the net expenditure incurred in the relevant analysis column. Using the above example, the amount paid on the taxi fare on 2 Jan was £9.60. Note that £9.60 is entered in the total payment column, £1.60 is entered in the VAT column and £8.00 entered in the travel column.

  Note that occasionally there may be more than one type of expense on a voucher, eg 'paperclips' and 'bleach'. In cases like this the total VAT (if there is any) is entered in the VAT column and the individual amounts entered in the appropriate analysis columns, in this example it will be the 'stationery' and 'cleaning' columns. The details column will list the individual expenses, eg 'paperclips, bleach.'

- At the end of the period each money column is added up.

- It is then important to cross-check the additions, ie the total of all the analysis columns should equal the total payments made. This process in accounting terms is known as to 'cross cast'. Using the example on the previous page the analysis columns totals are cross cast (added) as follows:

	£
VAT	6.16
Postage	32.50
Travel	13.00
Stationery	17.84
Refreshments	6.24
Total Payments	75.74

You will note that this total agrees with the total of the "Total Payments Column" ie £75.74.

- In the next chapter we shall see how the petty cash book is balanced and the imprest restored to the original float.

Chapter summary

- Entering transactions into the petty cash book starts with the opening balance.

- The amount received from the bank to restore the imprest is entered next.

- It is important to ensure that the petty cash vouchers have been completed correctly, that calculations are accurate and the vouchers are properly authorised prior to entry.

- The next step is to enter the petty cash vouchers into the petty cash book.

- Lastly, all the analysis columns in the petty cash book will be totalled and checked against the total payments column to ensure that they equal the total payments.

Key terms

opening balance	the amount of cash in the petty cash tin at the start of the period
analysis column	a column into which the types of expenditure – eg stationery, postage – are entered
cross-check	adding up figures in analysis columns and ensuring that they equal the total payment column, which should be added up separately (this process is also known as to 'cross cast' in accountancy terms)

Exercises

Answers to the asterisked questions are to be found at the back of this book.

10.1* (a) A business operates their petty cash using the imprest system. The float for the period is £100.00 and during the period a total of £42.16 is spent. How much cash would the petty cashier need to obtain from the main cashier to restore the imprest?

(b) Ms Ainsworth is the petty cashier in a small business. The petty cash is operated using the imprest system with a float of £250.00 for a monthly period. During May the total payments out of petty cash was £231.78.

Calculate the amount of cash that Ms Ainsworth will need to ask the main cashier for to restore the imprest to £250.00.

(c) John is the petty cashier at a local estate agents which operates their petty cash using the imprest system. The float for a monthly period is £75.00. During December the company sends out Christmas cards and calendars to clients and by the third week of the period John realises that all the petty cash for the month has been spent and he still has several claims to pay.

Advise John what he should do in these circumstances.

(d) A company operates their petty cash using the imprest system with a float of £50. At the end of the period they have £12.14 left in the cash box.

How much cash should the petty cashier claim from the accountant to restore the imprest?

10.2* You work as an accounts clerk for a local printing company and one of your tasks is to look after the petty cash.

You are asked to write up the petty cash book, page 18, for May 2011 using the following analysis columns: VAT, postage, cleaning, travel, stationery and sundry expenses.

The cash float brought down at the beginning of the month is shown below, and the next voucher number to use is 73.

2011		£
1 May	Petty cash float brought down	100.00
3 May	Paid for postage stamps (no VAT)	18.00
6 May	Bought envelopes (including VAT of 71p)	4.30
9 May	Train fare to Manchester (no VAT)	6.50
11 May	Donation to local charity (no VAT)	25.00
18 May	Postage on parcel to customer (no VAT)	5.74
23 May	Bought envelopes (including VAT of £1.53)	9.20
25 May	Window cleaner (no VAT)	8.00
30 May	Office cleaner (no VAT)	10.00

A suitable blank petty cash book page is provided on the next page. You may photocopy this page for use if you wish. Alternatively you may download blank forms from the Resources section of www.osbornebooks.co.uk or copy the blank form at the end of this book.

After entering the vouchers you are asked to total all the columns and cross-check to ensure that calculations have been carried out correctly.

State how much money is left at the end of May. What amount would the petty cashier need from the cashier to restore the imprest?

Petty Cash Book

Receipts		Date	Details	Voucher Number	Total Payments		VAT		Postage		Cleaning		Travel		Stationery		Sundry Expenses	
£	p				£	p	£	p	£	p	£	p	£	p	£	p	£	p

10.3* Prepare a petty cash book for Wildthorn Guest House with analysis columns for VAT, postage, cleaning, travel, stationery and sundry expenses.

A suitable blank petty cash book page is provided on the previous page. You may photocopy this page for use if you wish. Alternatively you may download blank forms from the Resources section of www.osbornebooks.co.uk or copy the blank form at the end of this book.

Enter the following authorised transactions for the month of March 2011 on page 34 of the petty cash book.

The voucher amounts include VAT at 20% unless stated otherwise.

2011

1 March	Cash Balance brought down £50.00
3 March	Office cleaner (no VAT) £15.00, voucher no 101
7 March	Postage stamps (no VAT) £4.50, voucher no 102
11 March	Flowers for reception £6.00, including VAT of £1.00, voucher no 103
16 March	Dusters, polish for cleaning £3.75, including VAT of 62p, voucher no 104
21 March	Bus fares (no VAT) £2.50, voucher no 105
28 March	Window cleaner (no VAT) £8.00, voucher no 106
31 March	Envelopes £2.30, pens £3.60, including total VAT of 98p, voucher no 107
31 March	Postage stamps 0.90p (no VAT), voucher no 108

At the end of the month total all columns and cross-check against the total expenses incurred for March. Indicate to the manager of the hotel the amount of cash required to restore the imprest to £50.00.

10.4* J. Dolan operates an analytical petty cash book using the imprest system. On 1 June 2011 there was an opening balance in the petty cash box of £26.80. As petty cashier you are asked to carry out the following tasks:

(a)   Enter the opening balance into the petty cash book on page 56.

(b)   Enter the correct amount of cash to restore the imprest to the original float of £100.00. Use cash book reference CB1.

(c)   Enter the details of the petty cash vouchers shown on pages 230-233 into the petty cash book using the following analysis columns, VAT, postage, cleaning, sundry expenses, stationery and refreshments.

(d)   Total and cross-check the petty cash book at the end of June.

(e)   State how much money the petty cashier would have left at the end of June and how much would be required to restore the imprest.

A blank petty cash book page is provided on the next page and also at the back of this book. You may photocopy this page for use if you wish. Alternatively you may download a copy from the Resources section of www.osbornebooks.co.uk

Petty Cash Book

Receipts £ p	Date	Details	Voucher Number	Total Payments £ p	VAT £ p	Postage £ p	Cleaning £ p	Sundry Expenses £ p	Stationery £ p	Refresh-ments £ p

petty cash voucher   No. 001

                                              date   1 June 2011

description		amount
	£	p
Milk (for visitors) no VAT	2	80
	2	80

signature   *J. Bond*

authorised   *GR*

---

petty cash voucher   No. 002

                                              date   3 June 2011

description		amount
	£	p
Coffee, tea bags and biscuits (for visitors) no VAT	6	13
	6	13

signature   *M. Franks*

authorised   *GR*

---

petty cash voucher   No. 003

                                              date 9 June 2011

description		amount
	£	p
Office cleaner (no VAT)	20	–
	20	–

signature   *M Bould*

authorised   *GR*

petty cash voucher   No. 004

date   16 June 2011

description		amount
	£	p
Marker pens	3	36
Dusters	1	32
(including VAT of 78p)		
	4	68

signature   _S. Scott_

authorised   _GR_

---

petty cash voucher   No. 005

date 24 June 2011

description		amount
	£	p
Postage stamps	10	50
Parcel post	3	42
(no VAT)	13	92

signature   _S. Scott_

authorised   _GR_

---

petty cash voucher   No. 006

date 24/6/2011

description		amount
	£	p
Donation to local junior football club (no VAT)	5	–
	5	–

signature   _S. Scott_

authorised   _GR_

petty cash voucher   No. 007

date 27/6/2011

description	amount	
	£	p
Window cleaner (no VAT)	10	–
	10	–

signature   M Bould

authorised   GR

---

petty cash voucher   No. 008

date 27 June 2011

description	amount	
	£	p
Envelopes	4	20
Copier paper	10	20
(including VAT)		
	14	40

signature   S. Scott

authorised   GR

---

petty cash voucher   No. 009

date 30 June 2011

description	amount	
	£	p
Bus fares to bank (no VAT)	2	30
	2	30

signature   D. Huntley

authorised   GR

petty cash voucher		No. 010
	date	30 June 2011

description		amount	
		£	p
Milk (office visitors) no VAT		2	38
		2	38

signature *Paul Brown*

authorised *GR*

petty cash voucher		No. 011
	date	30 June 2011

description		amount	
		£	p
Postage stamps (no VAT)		4	50
		4	50

signature *S. Scott*

authorised *GR*

10.5 As accounts assistant for Blake Business Products Ltd you are required to look after the petty cash book as one of your duties. On 1 September 2011 there was £12.36 left in the petty cash box from the previous month. The cashier, Joe Morgan, gives you £62.64 to restore the imprest to £75.00.

You are to:

(a) Enter the balance brought down from the previous month £12.36 together with the amount required to restore the imprest in the petty cash book, page 24, on 1 September 2011.

(b) Your next task is to enter the petty cash vouchers (shown on pages 236-239) for September 2011 in the petty cash book using the following analysis columns: VAT, postage, cleaning, travel, stationery and sundry expenses.

(c) At the end of September total all the columns and cross-check.

(d) State how much money the petty cashier would have left at the end of September and how much would be required to restore the imprest.

A suitable blank petty cash book page is provided on the next page. You may photocopy this page for your use if you wish. Alternatively you may download a copy from the Resources section of www.osbornebooks.co.uk

Petty Cash Book

Receipts £ p	Date	Details	Voucher Number	Total Payments £ p	VAT £ p	Postage £ p	Cleaning £ p	Travel £ p	Stationery £ p	Sundry Expenses £ p

petty cash voucher		No. 100
		date **1 Sept 2011**

description	amount	
	£	p
Postage stamps (no VAT)	4	20
	4	20

signature *Simon Duffy*

authorised *JB*

petty cash voucher		No. 101
		date **5 Sept 2011**

description	amount	
	£	p
Flowers for office reception including VAT of 62p	3	75
	3	75

signature *J. Davies*

authorised *JB*

petty cash voucher		No. 102
		date **8/9/2011**

description	amount	
	£	p
A4 copy paper Correcting fluid (incl VAT of £1.30)	7	80
	7	80

signature *M Noel*

authorised *JB*

petty cash voucher		No. 103
		date 9 Sept 2011

description	amount	
	£	p
Packing boxes (incl VAT of £2.40)	14	40
	14	40

signature _S. Scott_

authorised _GR_

petty cash voucher		No. 104
		date 12/9/11

description	amount	
	£	p
Parcel post (no VAT)	–	80
	–	80

signature _Simon Duffy_

authorised _JB_

petty cash voucher		No. 105
		date 13 Sept 2011

description	amount	
	£	p
4 Lever arch files	10	56
Toilet rolls	4	32
(incl VAT of £2.48)		
	14	88

signature _A Bell_

authorised _JB_

petty cash voucher   No. 106

date **15 Sept 2011**

description		amount	
		£	p
Bus fare to solicitors to collect documents (no VAT)		1	20
		1	20

signature _F Oddy_

authorised _JB_

---

petty cash voucher   No. 107

date **17/9/2011**

description		amount	
		£	p
Furniture polish (including VAT)		3	84
		3	84

signature _Ethel May_

authorised _JB_

---

petty cash voucher   No. 108

date **29/9/2011**

description		amount	
		£	p
Postage stamps (no VAT)		4	80
		4	80

signature _J. Davies_

authorised _JB_

petty cash voucher			No. 109

date 30/9/2011

description		amount	
		£	p
Milk (for use by visitors) no VAT		3	60
		3	60

signature *A Bell*

authorised *JB*

11 Balancing the petty cash book

what this chapter covers . . .

This chapter explains the following processes:

- balancing off the petty cash book using the imprest system to find out how much cash remains

- the reconciliation of the cash in hand with the balance in the petty cash book

- the completion of the 'Cash in hand' form

- the completion of a 'Petty cash reimbursement request'

- the entry of the reimbursement of the petty cash expenditure in the petty cash book

OCR assessment criteria covered

Unit M5: Maintaining petty cash records

3.1 Balance off the petty cash book using the imprest system

3.2 Reconcile the petty cash book with cash in hand

3.3 Prepare a petty cash reimbursement request or equivalent

3.4 Show the reimbursement of the petty cash expenditure in the petty cash book

BALANCING THE PETTY CASH BOOK

In the previous chapter the Case Study, 'Evans & Co', showed the entry of the petty cash vouchers into the petty cash book. In this chapter we are going to show how the petty cash book of 'Evans & Co' is totalled, balanced and the reimbursement of the petty cash expenditure entered.

The balance of cash left at the end of the period will then be counted and a **Cash in hand form** completed to ensure that the money in the cash box equals the balance as shown in the petty cash book.

Finally, a **petty cash reimbursement request** will be completed requesting cash to replace the amount of petty cash expenditure for the period. The reimbursement of the petty cash expenditure is then entered into the petty cash book.

balancing the account

In the Case Study 'Evans & Co', in the previous chapter (see pages 220-222), the total amount spent during the first week in January was £75.74. This figure was checked when the totals of all the analysis columns were added up and cross-checked as follows:

	£
VAT	6.16
Postage	32.50
Travel	13.00
Stationery	17.84
Refreshments	6.24
Total Payments	75.74

To balance the petty cash book at the end of the period it is necessary to add up the 'Receipts' column as follows (see also next page):

	£
Balance b/d	20.00
Cash	80.00
Total Receipts	100.00

Now that the totals of 'Receipts' and 'Payments' for the period are known the amount of the 'balance' can be found as follows (see also next page):

	£
Total receipts	100.00
Less total payments	75.74
Balance	24.26

The 'balance' figure £24.26 is the difference between the total receipts and the total payments and should be the amount of money that the petty cashier has left in the cash box. The balance figure is then entered in the petty cash book as shown below.

Petty Cash Book

Receipts £ p	Date	Details	Voucher Number	Total Payments £ p	VAT £ p	Postage £ p	Cleaning £ p	Motor Expenses £ p	Stationery £ p	Refresh-ments £ p
	2011									
20.00	1 Jan	Balance b/d								
80.00	1 Jan	Cash								
	2 Jan	Postage stamps	21	10.00		10.00				
	2 Jan	Taxi fare	22	9.60	1.60			8.00		
	3 Jan	Envelopes	23	8.40	1.40				7.00	
	4 Jan	Registered package	24	12.50		12.50				
	5 Jan	Office milk and tea	25	6.24						6.24
	6 Jan	Postage stamps	26	10.00		10.00				
	6 Jan	Suspension files	27	13.00	2.16				10.84	
	7 Jan	Taxi fare	28	6.00	1.00			5.00		
				75.74	6.16	32.50		13.00	17.84	6.24
100.00	7 Jan	Balance c/d		24.26						
				100.00						
24.26	8 Jan	Balance b/d								

entering the balances in the petty cash book

The balance of money left at the end of the period will be entered in the petty cash book, as shown opposite.

You will notice that the balance is shown twice, once as 'Balance c/d' which stands for 'Balance carried down' and also as 'Balance b/d' for 'Balance brought down'. This is normal accounting practice and indicates that the closing balance of one period becomes the opening balance for the next period.

reconciling the petty cash book with the cash in hand

At the end of a period, usually a week or month, the petty cashier balances the petty cash book and enters the balance of cash remaining in the petty cash book. Once this has been carried out the petty cashier needs to ensure that the 'balance' according to the petty cash book equals the amount of money held in the cash box. The money in the cash box will be counted and entered in a 'Cash in hand form' which is used to calculate the total:

CASH IN HAND FORM		Quantity	Total
Date			
Notes	£10		
	£5		
Coins	£2		
	£1		
	50p		
	20p		
	10p		
	5p		
	2p		
	1p		
Total			£

In our case study of Evans & Co the balance of cash left at the end of the period amounted to £24.26. The petty cashier will count the money in the cash box to make sure that the cash in hand equals the balance. The Cash in hand form is then completed as shown on the next page.

CASH IN HAND FORM			
Date 7 January 2011		Quantity	Total
Notes	£10		
	£5	2	£10.00
Coins	£2	2	£4.00
	£1	6	£6.00
	50p	4	£2.00
	20p	5	£1.00
	10p	10	£1.00
	5p	4	£0.20
	2p	2	£0.04
	1p	2	£0.02
Total			£24.26

If the money in the cash box equals the amount of the petty cash book balance then this is an indication that no errors have been made. If, however, the money held does not equal the amount of the balance, the petty cashier will need to check all the entries made into the petty cash book and recount the cash. If an error has been made it should be identified by carrying out these checks. In the above example, the two totals agree; the figure is £24.26.

COMPLETION OF PETTY CASH REIMBURSEMENT REQUEST

When the petty cash book has been balanced off, the petty cashier will know the amount of money required to restore the imprest to the original amount. In the above case the amount required was £75.74 to restore the imprest to £100.00 as shown below. In order to obtain the money the petty cashier will need to complete a Petty Cash Reimbursement Request, as shown on the next page. The calculation is shown below:

	£
Amount of float	100.00
Less balance of money left (see above)	24.26
Amount needed to restore the imprest	75.74

PETTY CASH REIMBURSEMENT REQUEST

Please arrange for a cheque for £ ___75.74___ to restore imprest.

Signed _Amy Bennett_ _____ Petty Cashier

entering the reimbursement in the petty cash book

The reimbursement of the petty cash expenditure, ie £75.74, should then be entered in the petty cash book, an extract from which is shown below:

Receipts £ p	Date	Details	Voucher Number	Total £ p
	2011			
24.26	8 Jan	Balance b/d		
75.74	8 Jan	Cash		

Chapter summary

- When all the entries for a period have been entered into the petty cash book the petty cashier 'balances' the account.

- The balance is then entered twice in the petty cash book, as 'balance c/d' and 'balance b/d'.

- The cash in hand is then counted and the 'Cash in hand' form completed to ensure that the total equals the 'balance'.

- A 'Petty cash reimbursement request' form is completed, requesting an amount of money from the cashier or accountant to enable the imprest to be restored to the original amount.

- The reimbursement of the petty cash expenditure into the petty cash book is shown.

Key terms

balancing the account	calculating the balance on the account by finding the difference between the total receipts and payments; the difference is the 'balance'
balance c/d	this stands for 'balance carried down' and is the balance on the account at the end of the period
balance b/d	this stands for 'balance brought down' and represents the amount or balance at the beginning of a new period

 **Exercises**

Answers to the asterisked questions are to be found at the back of this book.

11.1* You are employed as Accounts Assistant for Hulme Bros. Ltd. The company operates their petty cash book using the imprest system on a weekly basis with a float of £60.00. On 7 March 2011 there was £4.36 left in the petty cash box from the previous week.

The following are details of the petty cash vouchers for the week:

		£
7 March	Window cleaner (no VAT)	8.50
7 March	Postage stamps (no VAT)	4.50
8 March	Petrol (including VAT £3.60)	21.60
9 March	Coffee, tea and biscuits for visitors (no VAT)	5.70
9 March	Parcel post (no VAT)	3.60
10 March	Envelopes (including VAT)	4.08
11 March	Thick bleach (including VAT)	2.88

The cash held at the end of the week is as follows:

CASH IN HAND FORM			
Date		Quantity	Total
Notes	£10		
	£5	1	
Coins	£2		
	£1	2	
	50p	2	
	20p	3	
	10p	4	
	5p	2	
	2p	1	
	1p	2	
Total			£

A blank 'Petty cash book page', 'Cash in hand form', and 'Petty cash reimbursement request' are provided on the pages that follow and also at the end of this book. You may photocopy these forms if you wish. Alternatively you may download blank forms from the Resources section of www.osbornebooks.co.uk

Tasks:

(a)   Enter the opening balance into the petty cash book.

(b)   Enter the correct amount of cash which has been collected from the bank to restore the imprest to £60.00.

(c)   Enter the listed transactions into the petty cash book using the following analysis columns: VAT, postage, cleaning, motor expenses, stationery and refreshments. You may have to calculate some of the VAT which is charged at the standard rate of 20%.

The next voucher number to use is 42.

(d)   Total and cross cast the petty cash book.

(e)   Balance the petty cash book as at 11 March 2011 and bring down the balance ready for the week commencing 14 March 2011.

(f)   Complete a Cash in hand form using the details of cash shown on the form on the previous page and reconcile the total with the petty cash book balance.

(g)   Prepare the petty cash reimbursement request.

(h)   Show the reimbursement of the petty cash expenditure in the petty cash book.

CASH IN HAND FORM			
Date		Quantity	Total
Notes	£10		
	£5		
Coins	£2		
	£1		
	50p		
	20p		
	10p		
	5p		
	2p		
	1p		
Total			£

PETTY CASH REIMBURSEMENT REQUEST

Please arrange for a cheque for £ _____ to restore imprest.

Signed _____ Petty Cashier

Petty Cash Book

Receipts £ p	Date	Details	Voucher Number	Total Payments £ p	VAT £ p	Postage £ p	Cleaning £ p	Motor Expenses £ p	Stationery £ p	Refreshments £ p

11.2* As junior assistant in the offices of Chell Construction Co one of your duties is to look after the petty cash. The petty cash is operated using the imprest system with a float of £100.00 per month. On 3 January 2011 the balance of cash in hand brought down from December 2010 is £16.22.

(a) Enter the opening balance into the petty cash book (page 43).

(b) Enter the correct amount of cash which has been collected from the bank to restore the imprest to £100.00.

(c) Enter the transactions listed below into the petty cash book using the following analysis columns: VAT, postage, cleaning, motor expenses, stationery and sundry expenses. You may have to calculate some of the VAT which is charged at the standard rate of 20%.

The next voucher number to use is 27.

(d) Total and cross cast the petty cash book.

(e) Balance the petty cash book as at 31 January 2011 and bring down the balance ready for the next month starting 1 February 2011.

(f) Complete a Cash in hand form using the details shown on the form at the top of page 252 and reconcile the total with the petty cash book balance.

(g) Prepare the petty cash reimbursement request.

(h) Show the reimbursement of the petty cash expenditure in the petty cash book.

Details of transactions for January 2011:		£
3 January	Construction trade magazine for reception (no VAT)	3.30
4 January	Postage stamps (no VAT)	8.00
7 January	Petrol (including VAT of £4.00)	24.00
10 January	Parcel to London (no VAT)	4.20
13 January	1 Packet Document Wallets (including VAT)	4.56
14 January	Office cleaner (no VAT)	22.00
20 January	Copy paper (including VAT)	4.80
25 January	Postage stamps (no VAT)	4.00
27 January	Petrol (including VAT)	14.40

A blank 'Petty cash book page', 'Cash in hand form', and 'Petty cash reimbursement request' are provided on the pages that follow and also at the end of this book. You may photocopy these forms if you wish. Alternatively you may download blank forms from the Resources section of www.osbornebooks.co.uk

Petty Cash Book

Receipts £ p	Date	Details	Voucher Number	Total Payments £ p	VAT £ p	Postage £ p	Cleaning £ p	Motor expenses £ p	Stationery £ p	Sundry expenses £ p

Details of cash held at the end of the week:

CASH IN HAND FORM			
Date		Quantity	Total
Notes	£10		
	£5		
Coins	£2	2	
	£1	3	
	50p	3	
	20p	5	
	10p	10	
	5p	2	
	2p	5	
	1p	4	
Total			£

CASH IN HAND FORM			Quantity	Total
Date				
Notes		£10		
		£5		
Coins		£2		
		£1		
		50p		
		20p		
		10p		
		5p		
		2p		
		1p		
Total				£

PETTY CASH REIMBURSEMENT REQUEST

Please arrange for a cheque for £ _____ to restore imprest.

Signed _____ Petty Cashier

11.3* D Ashcroft Ltd operates an analytical petty cash book using the imprest system.

On 1 July 2011 there was an opening balance of £56.40. As petty cashier you are required to carry out the following tasks:

(a)   Enter the opening balance into the petty cash book on page 11.

(b)   Enter the correct amount of cash which has been collected from the bank to restore the imprest to £150.00.

(c)   Enter the details of the petty cash vouchers into the petty cash book on page 11 using the following analysis columns: VAT, postage, cleaning, motor expenses, stationery and refreshments. You may have to calculate some of the VAT which is charged at the standard rate of 20%.

(d)   Total and cross cast the petty cash book.

(e)   Balance the petty cash book on 31 July 2011 and bring down the balance ready for 1 August 2011.

(f)   Complete a Cash in hand form using the details shown on the form on page 259 and reconcile the total with the petty cash book balance.

(g)   Prepare the Petty cash reimbursement request form.

(h)   Enter the reimbursement of the petty cash expenditure in the petty cash book.

A blank 'Petty cash book page', 'Cash in hand form', and 'Petty cash reimbursement request' are provided on the pages that follow and also at the end of this book. You may photocopy these forms if you wish. Alternatively you may download blank forms from the Resources section of www.osbornebooks.co.uk

The petty cash vouchers are shown on the pages that follow:

petty cash voucher   No. 50

date   1 July 2011

description		amount
	£	p
Bleach	1	30
4 Files	12	00
VAT	2	66
	15	96

signature   *J Scott*

authorised   G Osborne

---

petty cash voucher   No. 51

date   4 July 2011

description		amount
	£	p
Petrol	21	60
(including VAT of £3.60)		
	21	60

signature   *Antony Morris*

authorised   G Osborne

---

petty cash voucher   No. 52

date   4 July 2011

description		amount
	£	p
Postage stamps (no VAT)	4	00
	4	00

signature   *J Scott*

authorised   G Osborne

petty cash voucher

No. 53

date 5 July 2011

description	amount	
	£	p
Window cleaner (no VAT)	15	-
	15	-

signature *Ada Wynn*

authorised G Osborne

petty cash voucher

No. 54

date 6 July 2011

description	amount	
	£	p
Tea, coffee and biscuits (no VAT)	5	32
	5	32

signature *J Scott*

authorised G Osborne

petty cash voucher

No. 55

date 11 July 2011

description	amount	
	£	p
Postage stamps (no VAT)	6	00
	6	00

signature *Bob Greaves*

authorised G Osborne

petty cash voucher   No. 56

                                            date   15 July 2011

description		amount	
		£	p
Petrol (including VAT of £3.20)		19	20
		19	20

signature   *Anthony Morris*

authorised   G Osborne

---

petty cash voucher   No. 57

                                            date   18 July 2011

description		amount	
		£	p
Chocolate biscuits for meeting (including VAT of £1.12)		6	72
		6	72

signature   *J Scott*

authorised   G Osborne

---

petty cash voucher   No. 58

                                            date   21 July 2011

description		amount	
		£	p
Photocopy paper (including VAT - amount not on receipt)		9	60
		9	60

signature   *J Scott*

authorised   G Osborne

petty cash voucher		No. 59
	date	25 July 2011

description	amount	
	£	p
Office cleaner (no VAT)	20	-
	20	-

signature _Ada Wynn_

authorised _G Osborne_

Details of cash held at the end of the week:

CASH IN HAND FORM			
Date		Quantity	Total
Notes	£10	1	
	£5	1	
Coins	£2	2	
	£1	3	
	50p	4	
	20p	10	
	10p	4	
	5p	2	
	2p	3	
	1p	4	
Total			£

CASH IN HAND FORM				
Date			Quantity	Total
	Notes	£10		
		£5		
	Coins	£2		
		£1		
		50p		
		20p		
		10p		
		5p		
		2p		
		1p		
	Total			£

PETTY CASH REIMBURSEMENT REQUEST

Please arrange for a cheque for £ _____ to restore imprest.

Signed _____ Petty Cashier

Petty Cash Book

Receipts £ p	Date	Details	Voucher Number	Total Payments £ p	VAT £ p	Postage £ p	Cleaning £ p	Motor Expenses £ p	Stationery £ p	Refreshments £ p

11.4 Fairacres Garden Centre operates an analytical petty cash book using the imprest system. On 1 June 2011 there was an opening balance in the petty cash box of £18.58.

As the Petty Cashier you are required to perform the following tasks:

(a) Enter the opening balance into the petty cash book on page 20.

(b) Enter the correct amount of cash which has been collected from the bank to restore the imprest to £150.00.

(c) Prepare the petty cash vouchers for the expenses listed below and calculate the VAT where it is included in the expenses. The standard rate of Value Added Tax (VAT) to be used in this exercise is 20%.

The next available petty cash voucher number is 72.

(d) Enter the petty cash vouchers in date order into the analysed petty cash book using the following analysis columns:

VAT, postage, stationery, refreshments and sundry expenses

Ensure any VAT paid on expenses is entered into the appropriate analysis column.

(e) Total and cross cast the petty cash book.

(f) Balance the petty cash book on 30 June 2011 and bring down the balance ready for the 1 July 2011.

(g) Complete a Cash in hand form using the details shown on the form on the next page and reconcile the total with the petty cash book balance.

(h) Prepare the petty cash reimbursement request.

(i) Enter the reimbursement of the petty cash expenditure in the petty cash book.

A blank 'Petty cash book page', 'Cash in hand form', and 'Petty cash reimbursement request' are provided on the pages that follow and also at the end of this book. You may photocopy these forms if you wish. Alternatively you may download blank forms from the Resources section of www.osbornebooks.co.uk

Details of the petty cash expenditures are as follows:

1 On 2 June 2011, Barbara Blinston was asked to purchase 2 balls of string costing £4.20 including VAT.

2 On 3 June 2011, Mary Lawson was asked to pay the milk bill of £8.60 (VAT zero rated) and purchase toilet rolls costing £12.00 including VAT.

3 On 8 June 2011, Fred Lee purchased petrol costing £30.00 including VAT.

4 On 16 June 2011, Jane Simpson was asked to purchase postage stamps costing £5.52 (no VAT) and a jar of coffee costing £3.80 (VAT zero rated).

5 On 22 June 2011, Terry Belfield was asked to purchase some envelopes costing £2.60 plus VAT and white card size A3 costing £13.40 plus VAT.

6 On 29 June 2011, Neil Patel was asked to pay for the postage on a parcel costing £7.45 (VAT exempt) and a box of pens costing £6.00 plus VAT £1.20.

Details of cash held at the end of the week:

CASH IN HAND FORM			
Date		Quantity	Total
Notes	£10	2	
	£5	4	
Coins	£2	3	
	£1	2	
	50p	4	
	20p	5	
	10p	5	
	5p	8	
	2p	5	
	1p	3	
Total			£

petty cash voucher			No.
		date	
description			amount
		£	p
signature			
authorised			

petty cash voucher No.

date

description   amount

	£	p

signature ....

authorised ....

petty cash voucher No.

date

description   amount

	£	p

signature ....

authorised ....

petty cash voucher No.

date

description   amount

	£	p

signature ....

authorised ....

petty cash voucher No.

date

description		amount
	£	p

signature ....

authorised ....

petty cash voucher No.

date

description		amount
	£	p

signature ....

authorised ....

Petty Cash Book

Receipts £ p	Date	Details	Voucher Number	Total Payments £ p	VAT £ p	Postage £ p	Stationery £ p	Refresh-ments £ p	Sundry Expenses £ p

CASH IN HAND FORM				
Date			Quantity	Total
Notes		£10		
		£5		
Coins		£2		
		£1		
		50p		
		20p		
		10p		
		5p		
		2p		
		1p		
Total				£

PETTY CASH REIMBURSEMENT REQUEST

Please arrange for a cheque for £ _____ to restore imprest.

Signed _____ Petty Cashier

answers to activities

These are the answers to the asterisked questions at the end of each chapter.

CHAPTER 1: PROCESSING DOCUMENTS FOR CREDIT SALES

1.1   B

1.3   B

1.5   A

1.6

INVOICE

Presto Supplies
18 Fencote Road, Worcester WR2 6HY
Tel 01905 334482 email info@prestosupplies.com
VAT Reg 987 5441 21

Alpha Stationery
34, High Street
Southbury
SY1 4DB

invoice number	12340
purchase order number	1066
date	14 December 2011

Quantity	Product code	Description	Unit price £	Total £
5	RBBU5	AlbaGel Rollerball, blue (5 pack)	4.95	24.75
5	CP1R	A4 Alba copy paper (250 pack)	2.95	14.75
2	DLWSS	DL Self-seal envelopes, white (100 pack)	3.95	7.90
		Sub-total		47.40
		VAT @ 20%		9.48
		Invoice total		56.88

terms:
Net 30 days

1.7

INVOICE

Presto Supplies
18 Fencote Road, Worcester WR2 6HY
Tel 01905 334482 email info@prestosupplies.com
VAT Reg 987 5441 21

Delphic Limited 34, Oracle Street Walvern WA1 7ST		

invoice number	12345
purchase order number	1951
date	15 December 2011

Quantity	Product code	Description	Unit price £	Total £
2	LAB01	1-Line Permanent Labels, white (6000 pack)	11.95	23.90
5	SNC6	Sticky Notes, 76x76mm, mixed colours (6 pack)	6.95	34.75
7	RBBK	2-ring PVC binder, A4, black	1.20	8.40
			Sub-total	67.05
			VAT @ 20%	13.41
			Invoice total	80.46

terms:
Net 30 days

1.9

CREDIT NOTE

Presto Supplies
18 Fencote Road, Worcester WR2 6HY
Tel 01905 334482 email info@prestosupplies.com
VAT Reg 987 5441 21

Alpha Stationery
34, High Street
Southbury
SY1 4DB

credit note number	946
purchase order number	1060
date	15 December 2011

Quantity	Product code	Description	Unit price £	Total £
2	PHB50	HB Pencils (50 pack)	3.45	6.90
			Sub-total	6.90
			VAT @ 20%	1.38
			Credit note total	8.28

Reason for return:
Goods missing from consignment

1.10

CREDIT NOTE

Presto Supplies
18 Fencote Road, Worcester WR2 6HY
Tel 01905 334482 email info@prestosupplies.com
VAT Reg 987 5441 21

Delphic Limited	
34, Oracle Street	
Walvern	
WA1 7ST	

credit note number	947
purchase order number	1945
date	15 December 2011

Quantity	Product code	Description	Unit price £	Total £
10	C4WSS	C4 Self-seal envelopes, white (250 pack)	24.00	240.00
5	SNY12	Sticky Notes, 76x76mm, yellow (12 pack)	9.95	49.75
		Sub-total		289.75
		VAT @ 20%		57.95
		Credit note total		347.70

Reason for return:
Goods damaged in transit

CHAPTER 2: PROCESSING SUPPLIER INVOICES AND CREDIT NOTES

2.1 C

2.3 A

2.5 A

2.6 Please note that credit note (d) from Presto Supplies is correct and so is not included on this list and can be processed.

Supplier	Purchase order number	Credit note number	Reason why credit note cannot be processed
(a) Zilon Computers	950	2703	Goods quantity differs Incorrect trade discount applied
(b) Droitwich Digital	955	1789	Product code and unit price differ Trade discount added on
(c) Delphic Limited	977	1924	Error in VAT calculation
(e) Zilon Computers	982	2732	Purchase order number differs Incorrect unit price Incorrect trade discount applied

CHAPTER 3: FROM DOCUMENTS TO DAYBOOKS

3.1

Purchase Day Book

Date	Details	Goods	VAT	Total
2011		£	£	£
24 Oct	J Miller Ltd	80.00	16.00	96.00
25 Oct	Hirst Supplies	168.00	33.60	201.60
27 Oct	Turner & Co	48.00	9.60	57.60
28 Oct	Manet Ltd	96.00	19.20	115.20
31 Oct	Total	392.00	78.40	470.40

Purchase Returns Day Book

Date	Details	Goods	VAT	Total
2011		£	£	£
26 Oct	J Macmillan	16.00	3.20	19.20
28 Oct	J Constable	64.00	12.80	76.80
31 Oct	Total	80.00	16.00	96.00

Sales Day Book

Date	Details	Goods	VAT	Total
2011		£	£	£
24 Oct	Coppola Ltd	304.00	60.80	364.80
26 Oct	J Mason	88.00	17.60	105.60
27 Oct	Cute Shop	120.00	24.00	144.00
28 Oct	P Casso	152.00	30.40	182.40
31 Oct	Total	664.00	132.80	796.80

Sales Returns Day Book

Date	Details	Goods	VAT	Total
2011		£	£	£
25 Oct	Coppola Ltd	56.00	11.20	67.20
27 Oct	J Steinbeck	72.00	14.40	86.40
31 Oct	Total	128.00	25.60	153.60

3.3

Purchase Day Book

Date	Details	Goods	VAT	Total
2011		£	£	£
21 Nov	AB Supplies	160.00	32.00	192.00
23 Nov	N Mehta Limited	322.80	64.56	387.36
28 Nov	AB Supplies	294.40	58.88	353.28
30 Nov	Total	777.20	155.44	932.64

Purchase Returns Day Book

Date	Details	Goods	VAT	Total
2011		£	£	£
25 Nov	AB Supplies	19.20	3.84	23.04
28 Nov	N Mehta Limited	28.80	5.76	34.56
30 Nov	Total	48.00	9.60	57.60

Sales Day Book

Date	Details	Goods	VAT	Total
2011		£	£	£
22 Nov	Gullwing Sports Ltd	320.00	64.00	384.00
23 Nov	Kerrison Sports	132.00	26.40	158.40
25 Nov	Gullwing Sports Ltd	225.00	45.00	270.00
28 Nov	Kerrison Sports	188.00	37.60	225.60
30 Nov	Total	865.00	173.00	1,038.00

Sales Returns Day Book

Date	Details	Goods	VAT	Total
2011		£	£	£
28 Nov	Gullwing Sports Ltd	60.00	12.00	72.00
29 Nov	Kerrison Sports	20.00	4.00	24.00
30 Nov	Total	80.00	16.00	96.00

CHAPTER 4: RECEIVING PAYMENTS

4.1

Receipts		
No	**Name**	**Amount £**
219	Briggs Services	65.20
220	Poole Trading	43.86
221	Marton Cars	151.12
222	Zhang Stores	33.50
223	Shah Mini-Market	12.76
224	Jones Joinery	53.13
		359.57

DAILY RECEIPTS LIST

Grant and Sons

Date   18 May 2011

Total Cash £ 359.57

4.2

TILL CONTENTS SHEET

Date 22 July 2011			Float		
Notes	**Quantity**	**Total**	**Notes**	**Quantity**	**Total**
£20	11	220.00	£20		
£10	8	80.00	£10		
£5	7	35.00	£5	2	10.00
Coins			**Coins**		
£2	9	18.00	£2	5	10.00
£1	31	31.00	£1	10	10.00
50p	14	7.00	50p	10	5.00
20p	16	3.20	20p	10	2.00
10p	24	2.40	10p	20	2.00
5p	13	0.65	5p	10	0.50
2p	28	0.56	2p	20	0.40
1p	15	0.15	1p	10	0.10
Cash Total		397.96	**Float Total**		40.00
			CASH TO BANK		357.96

DAILY RECEIPTS LIST

Monty's Music Shop

Date 22 July 2011

Total Cash £ 357.96

Date 22 July 2011   bank giro credit

Cashier's stamp

Western Bank
Southbury Branch

Account
Monty's Music Shop

Sort Code: 43 21 85
Account Number 07981534

Please do not write or mark below this line

£50 notes		
£20 notes	220	00
£10 notes	80	00
£5 notes	25	00
£2 coins	8	00
£1 coins	21	00
50p & 20p coins	3	20
10p & 5p coins	0	55
2p and 1p coins	0	21
Total Cash	**357**	**96**
Cheques etc (see overleaf)		
£	357	96

4.4 (a) Payee name incorrect, cheque out of date, cheque not signed, amount in words and figures differs

(b) Amount in words and figures differs

(c) Out of date, amount in words and figures differs

4.5

Customer	Cheque number	Reason cheque is not valid
Beech & Partners	136317	Amount in words does not agree with amount in figures
Thompson Ltd	234810	Cheque has not been signed

OUTSTANDING INVOICE LIST – September 2011

Customer	Invoice number	Invoice date	Amount £	Date payment received	Method of payment	Payment valid Yes/No
Beech & Partners	520	03.08.11	76.89	13.09.11	Cheque	No
Beech & Partners	528	05.08.11	133.40			
Cheshire Printing	511	01.08.11	52.16	07.09.11	Cheque	Yes
Greyfriars Ltd	530	11.08.11	180.60	16.09.11	BACS	Yes
Huang Services	529	11.08.11	315.20	13.09.11	Cheque	Yes
Kisicki & Son	531	15.08.11	526.00	21.09.11	Cheque	Yes
Kisicki & Son	533	18.08.11	39.72	29.09.11	Cheque	Yes
Radford Electrics	532	17.08.11	92.51	27.09.11	BGC	Yes
Thompson Ltd	534	23.08.11	74.53	29.09.11	Cheque	No
Thompson Ltd	527	10.08.11	163.35			

Total £	1,654.36

Account	Cedar Associates			Date	30 September 2011		
Cheques				**Cheques**			
				Cheshire Printing		52	16
				Huang Services		315	20
				Kisicki and Son		526	00
				Kisicki and Son		39	72
				Total carried overleaf	£	933	08

Date 30 Sept 2011   **bank giro credit**

Cashier's
stamp

Western Bank
Southbury Branch

Account
Cedar Associates

Sort Code: 28 03 47
Account Number 62405185

Please do not write or mark below this line

£50 notes		
£20 notes		
£10 notes		
£5 notes		
£2 coins		
£1 coins		
50p & 20p coins		
10p & 5p coins		
2p and 1p coins		
Total Cash		
Cheques etc (see overleaf)	933	08
£	933	08

CHAPTER 5: MAKING PAYMENTS

5.1

CASH REQUEST SLIP

Date   25 July 2011

Supplier   Jay's Office Supplies

To pay invoice no.   227

Notes	Quantity	Total *(£)*
£20		
£10	1	10.00
£5		
Coins		
£2	2	4.00
£1		
50p	1	0.50
20p	1	0.20
10p		
5p	1	0.05
2p	1	0.02
1p	1	0.01
Cash Total		14.78

5.3

REMITTANCE ADVICE
Nimrod Drainage

Unit 6, Riverside Park, Mereford, MR4 5TF
Tel 01908 761200 Fax 01908 761900
VAT REG GB 0745 8383 46

to   Mercia Wholesalers
     Unit 12
     Riverside Industrial Park
     Mereford
     MR2 7GH

date **28 April 2011**

order number   **C124/C172**

Invoice No	Date	Cheque No	Amount (£)
5517	16.03.11	000451	765.25
5792	01.04.11	000451	3,567.80
		TOTAL PAYMENT	**4,333.05**

Date 28.04.11

Mercia
Wholesalers

£ 4333.05

National Bank PLC
Mereford Branch
10 Cathedral Street, Mereford, MR1 5DE

Date 28 April 2011

35-09-75

Pay   Mercia Wholesalers

Four thousand three hundred and thirty three pounds

and five pence

£ 4,333.05

A/c payee only

NIMROD DRAINAGE LIMITED
Director   Director

000451   000451   35 09 75   12034875

CHAPTER 6: SOURCE DOCUMENTS FOR THE CASH BOOK

6.1

Cash Book (receipts side)

	Date	Details	Cash £ p	Bank £ p
	2011			
(a)	12 May	Cash sales	20.50	
	12 May	VAT – cash sales	4.10	
(b)	13 May	Cash sales	30.70	
	13 May	VAT – cash sales	6.14	
(c)	13 May	T F Retail		376.00
(d)	13 May	Y Goldsmith		487.50
(e)	13 May	Swingway Limited		95.00
(f)	13 May	Trendtime		196.00
(g)	13 May	R S Davies		156.50
(h)	13 May	Patricia Smith		97.50

6.2

Cash Book (payments side)

	Date	Details	Cheque Number	Cash £ p	Bank £ p
	2011				
(a)	24 May	Cash purchases		75.00	
	24 May	VAT – cash purchases		15.00	
(b)	25 May	Cash purchases		20.00	
	25 May	VAT – cash purchases		4.00	
(c)	25 May	Cash purchases		10.00	
	25 May	VAT – cash purchases		2.00	
(d)	20 May	R S Thomas	212345		200.00
(e)	20 May	G M Hopkins	212346		190.00
(f)	20 May	J Keats Ltd	212347		341.25
(g)	20 May	R Graves & Co	212348		380.00
(h)	20 May	W Owen	212349		245.95
(i)	20 May	W Blake Ltd	212350		71.25
(j)	23 May	T Hughes	212351		76.00
(k)	23 May	T Hardy Insurance	212352		140.40
(l)	23 May	S Plath & Associates	212353		195.00

CHAPTER 7: WRITING UP AND BALANCING THE CASH BOOK

7.1

Cash Book – Shaw Products

Date	Details	Cash £ p	Bank £ p	Date	Details	Cheque Number	Cash £ p	Bank £ p
2011								
Oct 1	Balance b/d	136.12	1,206.10					
Oct 7	Rose Services		260.00					
Oct 14	Image Designs		615.73					
Oct 14	Pollard Products		141.20					
Oct 21	Yung Wong & Co		417.38					
Oct 21	Peter James		72.60					
Oct 31	Keetz & Sons		170.00					
Oct 12	Cash Sales	120.00						
Oct 12	VAT – cash sales	24.00						
Oct 20	Cash Sales	37.80						
Oct 20	VAT – cash sales	7.56						

7.2

Cash Book – Clover Designs

Date	Details	Cheque Number	Cash £ p	Bank £ p
2011				
May 13	Charles Edge Ltd	508921		521.30
May 13	May & Co.	508922		79.40
May 13	M Singh Ltd	508923		721.80
May 31	Taylor Bros.	508924		92.75
May 31	Bond Paper Co	508925		201.50
May 31	Wang Stationers	508926		57.33
May 11	Cash Purchases		118.80	
May 11	VAT – cash purchases		23.76	
May 24	Cash Purchases		24.56	
May 24	VAT – cash purchases		4.91	

Date	Details	Cash £ p	Bank £ p

7.3

Cash Book – Spencer's Office Supplies

Date	Details	Cash £ p	Bank £ p
2011			
Mar 1	Balance b/d	235.00	2,345.00
Mar 4	Peak Dental Practice		44.85
Mar 4	Rippon (Estate Agents)		79.00
Mar 9	Premier Garage		144.25
Mar 11	Cash sales	92.30	
Mar 11	VAT – cash sales	18.46	
Mar 18	Halls Ltd		106.00
Mar 25	Cash sales	67.00	
Mar 25	VAT – cash sales	13.40	
Mar 30	Cash sales	123.00	
Mar 30	VAT – cash sales	24.60	
Mar 31	Cash sales	82.60	
Mar 31	VAT – cash sales	16.52	
		672.88	2,719.10
Apr 1	Balance b/d	603.40	908.35

Date	Details	Cheque Number	Cash £ p	Bank £ p
2011				
Mar 3	Cash purchases		40.00	
Mar 3	VAT – cash purchases		8.00	
Mar 11	Cash purchases		17.90	
Mar 11	VAT – cash purchases		3.58	
Mar 15	Office Supplies Ltd	925001		750.75
Mar 16	Cox & Co	925002		550.00
Mar 25	K Marsh	925003		110.00
Mar 30	Lomas Bros	925004		400.00
Mar 31	Balance c/d		603.40	908.35
			672.88	2,719.10

CHAPTER 8 – BANK RECONCILIATION STATEMENTS

8.1 FERN LIMITED

CASH BOOK (Bank columns only)					
RECEIPTS			PAYMENTS		
Date	Details	Bank	Date	Details	Bank
2011		£	2011		£
31 Aug	Balance b/d	2,284	31 Aug	Bank charges	55
30 Aug	Torr Bros (BGC)	92	31 Aug	City Finance (SO)	1,000
			31 Aug	Balance c/d	1,321
		2,376			2,376
1 Sep	Balance b/d	1,321			

FERN LIMITED
Bank Reconciliation Statement as at 31 August 2011

		£	£
Balance at bank as per Cash Book			1,321
Add: unpresented cheque(s)			
	Harvey & Co	206	
	Hill Bros	22	
	Ashleys Ltd	137	
			365
			1,686
Less: outstanding lodgement(s)		520	
		82	
			602
Balance at bank as per bank statement			1,084

8.2   BROOKLYN LIMITED

CASH BOOK (Bank columns only)						
RECEIPTS			PAYMENTS			
Date	Details	Bank	Date	Details		Bank
2011		£	2011			£
28 Feb	Balance b/d	705	26 Feb	Rates (DD)		103
27 Feb	D Stead (BACS)	220	28 Feb	Bank charges		38
			28 Feb	Balance c/d		784
		925				925
1 Mar	Balance b/d	784				

BROOKLYN LIMITED
Bank Reconciliation Statement as at 28 February 2011

	£	£
Balance at bank as per Cash Book		784
Add: unpresented cheque(s)		
R Jackson Ltd	540	
Spencer Partners	42	
Shanklin Garage	110	
White & Co	120	
		812
		1,596
Less: outstanding lodgement		94
Balance at bank as per bank statement		1,502

8.3   O'CONNOR LIMITED

	CASH BOOK (Bank columns only)					
	RECEIPTS				PAYMENTS	
Date	Details	Bank	Date	Details		Bank
2011		£	2011			£
28 Oct	Bayley's (BACS)	114	30 Oct	Balance b/d		604
31 Oct	Balance c/d	588	29 Oct	Bank interest		53
			29 Oct	Bank charges		45
		702				702
			1 Nov	Balance b/d		588

O'CONNOR LIMITED
Bank Reconciliation Statement as at 31 October 2011

	£	£
Balance at bank as per Cash Book		(588)
Add: unpresented cheque(s)		
Kerr's Garage	32	
J Choudrey	28	
	60	
		(528)
Less: outstanding lodgement(s)	58	
	209	
	267	
Balance at bank as per bank statement		(795)

CHAPTER 9: PRINCIPLES OF PETTY CASH

9.1 (a) Photocopier paper   pay from petty cash

(b) Office cleaner   item over the £25 limit, accountant to pay by cheque

(c) Parcel post   pay from petty cash

(d) Secretary's train ticket   personal expense – cannot be paid out of petty cash

(e) Tea, sugar and milk   pay from petty cash as these items are for visitors use

(f) Coffee for staff   coffee for staff use – cannot be paid out of petty cash

(g) Postage stamps   pay from petty cash

(h) Card, fabric, staples   item over the £25 limit, accountant to pay by cheque

(i) Job advert in local press   pay from petty cash

(j) Flowers for reception area   pay from petty cash

9.2 Morgan's Garage Ltd

Petty Cash Procedures – Brief Notes for Louise

- At the start of the new period make sure your petty cash balance equals the amount of cash in the petty cash box – do check by counting the cash in the petty cash box.

- Keep the petty cash box locked and keep the key in a safe place. Remember to put the petty cash box in the safe when not in use and especially each night on leaving the office.

- When making payments:

1   Make sure that the person making the claim has completed the petty cash voucher correctly and if possible supplied a receipt. Check all calculations.

2   The voucher must be signed by the person making the claim and to whom the money will be paid.

3   Check that the voucher has been authorised for payment by John Morgan.

- Enter the voucher details in the petty cash book. Remember to enter the VAT in the VAT column (if appropriate) and the expense under the relevant column.

- File the petty cash vouchers in number order.

- At the end of the month you will need to add up the amount of money spent during the month and claim this amount back from the accountant. See example below:

	£	
Our float for the month is	200.00	
Assume we spend	160.00	during the month
Amount left over	40.00	

If you add up the money left in the petty cash box it should equal £40.00.

You will then have to ask the accountant for £160.00 cash to make the float back up to £200.00 for the next month. Hopefully I should be back at work at the end of the month and will complete the balancing off procedures.

Best of Luck,

James

9.3

petty cash voucher   No. 22

date **today**

description		amount

	£	p
Postage stamps (no VAT)	18	30

Documentation will be a receipt from the Post Office for £18.30

	18	30

signature _Louise Carter_

authorised _A Student_

petty cash voucher   No. 23

date **today**

description		amount

	£	p
2 computer memory sticks @ £4.80 each includes total VAT of £1.60	9	60

Documentation will be a till receipt from stationery shop for £9.60

	9	60

signature _Martin Gould_

authorised _A Student_

petty cash voucher   No. 24

date **today**

description		amount

	£	p
Train fare to London to attend Health and Safety conference (no VAT)	35	00

Documentation will be a receipt from the train company for £35.00 or the train ticket.

	35	00

signature _C Edge_

authorised _Bob Allen_

9.5   Bode Manufacturers Ltd

	Total	VAT	Expense
	£	£	£
(a)	21.60	3.60	18.00
(b)	2.40	40p	2.00
(c)	8.58	1.43	7.15
(d)	1.44	24p	1.20
(e)	16.32	2.72	13.60
(f)	3.37	56p	2.81
(g)	92p	15p	77p
(h)	7.92	1.32	6.60
(i)	10.32	1.72	8.60
(j)	14.40	2.40	12.00

CHAPTER 10: WRITING UP THE PETTY CASH BOOK

			£
10.1	(a)	Petty cash float	100.00
		Less: Amount spent during the period	42.16
		Cash in hand	57.84
		Amount required to restore the imprest	42.16

			£
	(b)	Petty cash float	250.00
		Less: Amount spent during May	231.78
		Cash in hand	18.22
		Amount required to restore the imprest	231.78

(c) Since the petty cash float of £75.00 is not enough for the expenses John has to pay during December, more money will be needed. John will have to put in a request to the main cashier for the float to be increased from £75.00 to the amount required to cover the expenses for December. After these have been paid the float can return to the original amount or if John thinks the existing float is too small it may be necessary to increase the float permanently.

			£
	(d)	Petty cash float	50.00
		Amount left over for month	12.14
		Amount required to restore the imprest	37.86

10.2   Printing Company

Petty Cash Book

PCB 18

Receipts £ p	Date	Details	Voucher Number	Total Payments £ p	VAT £ p	Postage £ p	Cleaning £ p	Travel £ p	Stationery £ p	Sundry expenses £ p
100.00	2011 1 May	Balance b/d								
	3 May	Postage stamps	73	18.00		18.00				
	6 May	Envelopes	74	4.30	0.71				3.59	
	9 May	Train fare	75	6.50				6.50		
	11 May	Donation	76	25.00						25.00
	18 May	Parcel post	77	5.74		5.74				
	23 May	Envelopes	78	9.20	1.53				7.67	
	25 May	Window cleaner	79	8.00			8.00			
	30 May	Office cleaner	80	10.00			10.00			
				86.74	2.24	23.74	18.00	6.50	11.26	25.00
100.00										

Amount of cash left at the end of May is (£100.00 − £86.74) = £13.26

Amount required to restore the imprest is (£100.00 − £13.26) = £86.74

10.3   Wildthorn Guest House

Petty Cash Book

PCB 34

Receipts £ p	Date	Details	Voucher Number	Total Payments £ p	VAT £ p	Postage £ p	Cleaning £ p	Travel £ p	Stationery £ p	Sundry expenses £ p
50.00	2011 1 March	Balance b/d								
	3 March	Office cleaner	101	15.00			15.00			
	7 March	Postage stamps	102	4.50		4.50				
	11 March	Flowers	103	6.00	1.00					5.00
	16 March	Dusters and polish	104	3.75	0.62		3.13			
	21 March	Bus fares	105	2.50				2.50		
	28 March	Window cleaner	106	8.00			8.00			
	31 March	Envelopes & pens	107	5.90	0.98				4.92	
	31 March	Postage stamps	108	0.90		0.90				
50.00				46.55	2.60	5.40	26.13	2.50	4.92	5.00

Amount of cash required to restore the imprest = £46.55

10.4　J Dolan

Petty Cash Book

PCB 56

Receipts £ p	Date	Details	Voucher Number	Total Payments £ p	VAT £ p	Postage £ p	Cleaning £ p	Sundry expenses £ p	Stationery £ p	Refreshments £ p
	2011									
26.80	1 June	Balance b/d								
73.20	1 June	Cash	CB1							
	1 June	Milk	001	2.80						2.80
	3 June	Coffee, tea & biscuits	002	6.13						6.13
	9 June	Office cleaner	003	20.00			20.00			
	16 June	Marker pens & dusters	004	4.68	0.78		1.10		2.80	
	24 June	Stamps & parcel post	005	13.92		13.92				
	24 June	Donation (football club)	006	5.00				5.00		
	27 June	Window cleaner	007	10.00			10.00			
	27 June	Disks and ink cartridge	008	14.40	2.40				12.00	
	30 June	Bus fare	009	2.30				2.30		
	30 June	Milk	010	2.38						2.38
	30 June	Postage stamps	011	4.50		4.50				
				86.11	3.18	18.42	31.10	7.30	14.80	11.31
100.00										

Amount of cash left at 30 June is £100.00 – £86.11 = £13.89
Amount required to restore the imprest is £100.00 – £13.89 = £86.11

CHAPTER 11: BALANCING THE PETTY CASH BOOK

11.1a - e, h

Petty Cash Book 11.1 Hulme Bros Ltd PCB 12

Receipts £ p	Date	Details	Voucher Number	Total Payments £ p	VAT £ p	Postage £ p	Cleaning £ p	Motor expenses £ p	Stationery £ p	Refreshments £ p
		2011								
4.36	7 March	Balance b/d								
55.64	7 March	Bank	CB12							
	7 March	Window cleaner	42	8.50			8.50			
	7 March	Postage	43	4.50		4.50				
	8 March	Petrol	44	21.60	3.60			18.00		
	9 March	Coffee, tea & biscuits	45	5.70						5.70
	9 March	Parcel post	46	3.60		3.60				
	10 March	Envelopes	47	4.08	0.68				3.40	
	11 March	Thick bleach	48	2.88	0.48		2.40			
				50.86	4.76	8.10	10.90	18.00	3.40	5.70
60.00	11 March	Balance c/d		9.14						
				60.00						
9.14	14 March	Balance b/d								
50.86	14 March	Bank								

11.1f

CASH IN HAND FORM			
Date		Quantity	Total
Notes	£10		
	£5	1	5.00
Coins	£2		
	£1	2	2.00
	50p	2	1.00
	20p	3	0.60
	10p	4	0.40
	5p	2	0.10
	2p	1	0.02
	1p	2	0.02
Total			£ 9.14

11.1g

PETTY CASH REIMBURSEMENT REQUEST

Please arrange for a cheque for £ ___50.86___ to restore imprest.

Signed ___Candidate's name___ Petty Cashier

11.2 Chell Construction Co

11.2a - e, h

Petty Cash Book

PCB 43

Receipts £ p	Date	Details	Voucher Number	Total Payments £ p	VAT £ p	Postage £ p	Cleaning £ p	Motor expenses £ p	Stationery £ p	Sundry expenses £ p
	2011									
16.22	3 Jan	Balance b/d								
83.78	3 Jan	Bank								
	3 Jan	Trade magazine	27	3.30						3.30
	4 Jan	Postage stamps	28	8.00		8.00				
	7 Jan	Petrol	29	24.00	4.00			20.00		
	10 Jan	Parcel post	30	4.20		4.20				
	13 Jan	Document wallets	31	4.56	0.76				3.80	
	14 Jan	Office cleaner	32	22.00			22.00			
	20 Jan	Copy paper	33	4.80	0.80				4.00	
	25 Jan	Postage stamps	34	4.00		4.00				
	27 Jan	Petrol	35	14.40	2.40			12.00		
				89.26	7.96	16.20	22.00	32.00	7.80	3.30
	31 Jan	Balance c/d		10.74						
100.00				100.00						
10.74	1 Feb	Balance b/d								
89.26	1 Feb	Bank								

11.2f

CASH IN HAND FORM			
Date		Quantity	Total
Notes	£10		
	£5		
Coins	£2	2	4.00
	£1	3	3.00
	50p	3	1.50
	20p	5	1.00
	10p	10	1.00
	5p	2	0.10
	2p	5	0.10
	1p	4	0.04
Total		£	10.74

11.2g

PETTY CASH REIMBURSEMENT REQUEST

Please arrange for a cheque for £ __89.26__ to restore imprest.

Signed ___Candidate's name___ Petty Cashier

11.3 D Ashcroft Ltd

11.3a - e, h

Petty Cash Book

PCB 11

Receipts £ p	Date	Details	Voucher Number	Total Payments £ p	VAT £ p	Postage £ p	Cleaning £ p	Motor expenses £ p	Stationery £ p	Refreshments £ p
	2011									
56.40	1 July	Balance b/d								
93.60	1 July	Bank								
	1 July	Bleach and files	50	15.96	2.66		1.30			
	4 July	Petrol	51	21.60	3.60			18.00		
	4 July	Postage stamps	52	4.00		4.00				
	5 July	Window cleaner	53	15.00			15.00			
	6 July	Tea, coffee & biscuits	54	5.32						5.32
	11 July	Postage stamps	55	6.00		6.00				
	15 July	Petrol	56	19.20	3.20			16.00		
	18 July	Chocolate biscuits	57	6.72	1.12					5.60
	21 July	Photocopy paper	58	9.60	1.60				8.00	
	25 July	Office cleaner	59	20.00			20.00			
				123.40	12.18	10.00	36.30	34.00	20.00	10.92
26.60	31 July	Balance c/d		26.60						
150.00				150.00						
26.60	1 Aug	Balance b/d								
123.40	1 Aug	Bank								

11.3f

CASH IN HAND FORM			
Date		Quantity	Total
Notes	£10	1	10.00
	£5	1	5.00
Coins	£2	2	4.00
	£1	3	3.00
	50p	4	2.00
	20p	10	2.00
	10p	4	0.40
	5p	2	0.10
	2p	3	0.06
	1p	4	0.04
Total			£ 26.60

11.3g

PETTY CASH REIMBURSEMENT REQUEST

Please arrange for a cheque for £ _123.40_ to restore imprest.

Signed _____Candidate's name_____ Petty Cashier

document bank – photocopiable documents

The blank documents in this resource 'bank'

- may be photocopied by students and tutors for study purposes
- follow the order of the chapters and questions in this book
- are also available for download from the Resources section of www.osbornebooks.co.uk
- are the copyright © of Osborne Books Limited

Chapter 1 resources

INVOICE

Presto Supplies
18 Fencote Road, Worcester WR2 6HY
Tel 01905 334482 email info@prestosupplies.com
VAT Reg 987 5441 21

invoice number

purchase order number

date

Quantity	Product code	Description	Unit price £	Total £

			Sub-total	
			VAT @ 20%	
			Invoice total	

terms:
Net 30 days

Chapter 1 resources

CREDIT NOTE

Presto Supplies
18 Fencote Road, Worcester WR2 6HY
Tel 01905 334482 email info@prestosupplies.com
VAT Reg 987 5441 21

credit note number

purchase order number

date

Quantity	Product code	Description	Unit price £	Total £

			Sub-total	
			VAT @ 20%	
			Credit note total	

Reason for return:

Chapter 3 resources

Sales Day Book

Date	Details		Goods	VAT	Total

Sales Returns Day Book

Date	Details		Goods	VAT	Total

Chapter 3 resources

Purchase Day Book

Date	Details		Goods	VAT	Total

Purchase Returns Day Book

Date	Details	Goods	VAT	Total

Chapter 4 resources

DAILY RECEIPTS SLIP

_____

Date

Total Cash £

TILL CONTENTS SHEET

Date			Float		
Notes	**Quantity**	**Total**	**Notes**	**Quantity**	**Total**
£20			£20		
£10			£10		
£5			£5		
Coins			**Coins**		
£2			£2		
£1			£1		
50p			50p		
20p			20p		
10p			10p		
5p			5p		
2p			2p		
1p			1p		
Cash Total			**Float Total**		
			CASH TO BANK		

Chapter 4 resources

<table>
<tr><td colspan="4">Date_____   bank giro credit</td></tr>
<tr><td rowspan="13">Cashier's stamp

Western Bank
Southbury Branch

Account
Monty's Music Shop

Sort Code: 43 21 85
Account Number 07981534

Please do not write or mark below this line</td><td>£50 notes</td><td></td><td></td></tr>
<tr><td>£20 notes</td><td></td><td></td></tr>
<tr><td>£10 notes</td><td></td><td></td></tr>
<tr><td>£5 notes</td><td></td><td></td></tr>
<tr><td>£2 coins</td><td></td><td></td></tr>
<tr><td>£1 coins</td><td></td><td></td></tr>
<tr><td>50p & 20p coins</td><td></td><td></td></tr>
<tr><td>10p & 5p coins</td><td></td><td></td></tr>
<tr><td>2p and 1p coins</td><td></td><td></td></tr>
<tr><td>**Total Cash**</td><td></td><td></td></tr>
<tr><td>Cheques etc (see overleaf)</td><td></td><td></td></tr>
<tr><td>£</td><td></td><td></td></tr>
</table>

<table>
<tr><td colspan="4">Date_____   bank giro credit</td></tr>
<tr><td rowspan="13">Cashier's stamp

Western Bank
Southbury Branch

Account
Aztec Toys

Sort Code: 28 04 35
Account Number 44972067

Please do not write or mark below this line</td><td>£50 notes</td><td></td><td></td></tr>
<tr><td>£20 notes</td><td></td><td></td></tr>
<tr><td>£10 notes</td><td></td><td></td></tr>
<tr><td>£5 notes</td><td></td><td></td></tr>
<tr><td>£2 coins</td><td></td><td></td></tr>
<tr><td>£1 coins</td><td></td><td></td></tr>
<tr><td>50p & 20p coins</td><td></td><td></td></tr>
<tr><td>10p & 5p coins</td><td></td><td></td></tr>
<tr><td>2p and 1p coins</td><td></td><td></td></tr>
<tr><td>**Total Cash**</td><td></td><td></td></tr>
<tr><td>Cheques etc (see overleaf)</td><td></td><td></td></tr>
<tr><td>£</td><td></td><td></td></tr>
</table>

Chapter 4 resources

Customer	Cheque number	Reason cheque is not valid

Account				Date			
Cheques				Cheques			
				Total carried overleaf	£		

Date _____	bank giro credit		
Cashier's stamp	£50 notes		
	£20 notes		
Western Bank	£10 notes		
Southbury Branch	£5 notes		
	£2 coins		
Account	£1 coins		
Cedar Associates	50p & 20p coins		
	10p & 5p coins		
	2p and 1p coins		
Sort Code: 28 03 47	**Total Cash**		
Account Number 62405185	Cheques etc (see overleaf)		
Please do not write or mark below this line		£	

Chapter 5 resources

CASH REQUEST SLIP

Date _____

Supplier _____

To pay invoice no. _____

Notes	Quantity	Total (£)
£20		
£10		
£5		
Coins		
£2		
£1		
50p		
20p		
10p		
5p		
2p		
1p		
Cash Total		

Chapter 5 resources

REMITTANCE ADVICE
Nimrod Drainage
Unit 6, Riverside Park, Mereford, MR4 5TF
Tel 01908 761200 Fax 01908 761900
VAT REG GB 0745 8383 46

to		date	
		order number	

Invoice No.	Date	Cheque No.	Amount (£)
		TOTAL PAYMENT	

Date	**National Bank PLC**	Date	35-09-75

Mereford Branch
10 Cathedral Street, Mereford, MR1 5DE

Pay

Pay

A/c payee only

£

NIMROD DRAINAGE LIMITED
Director   Director

£

000451   000451   35 09 75   12034875

Chapter 5 resources

REMITTANCE ADVICE
Presto Supplies

18 Fencote Road, Worcester WR2 6HY
Tel 01905 334482 email: info@prestosupplies.com
VAT REG GB 987 5441 21

to

date _____

order number _____

Invoice No.	Date		Cheque No.	Amount (£)
			TOTAL PAYMENT	

Date _____

Pay

£ [ ]

126482

Southern Bank PLC
Mereford Branch
16 Broad Street, Mereford, MR1 7TR

Date _____

Pay

A/c payee only

£ [ ]

PRESTO SUPPLIES

97-76-54

126482   97 76 54   34284

Chapter 6 resources

Cash Book (receipts side)

Date	Details	Cash £ p	Bank £ p

Chapter 6 resources

Cash Book (payments side)

Date	Details	Cheque Number	Cash £ p	Bank £ p

Chapter 7 resources

Cash Book

Date	Details	Cheque Number	Cash £ p	Bank £ p

Date	Details	Cash £ p	Bank £ p

Chapter 8 resources

name of
business...

Bank Reconciliation Statement as at ....

	£	£
Balance at bank as per Cash Book		....
Add: unpresented cheque(s)		
	....	
		....
Less: outstanding lodgement(s)		
	....	
		....
Balance at bank as per bank statement		....

Note
Negative bank balances (ie overdrafts) should be shown in brackets.

Chapter 9 resources

petty cash voucher		No.
	date	
description		amount
	£	p
signature		
authorised		

petty cash voucher		No.
	date	
description		amount
	£	p
signature		
authorised		

petty cash voucher		No.
	date	
description		amount
	£	p
signature		
authorised		

Chapter 10 and 11 resources

Petty Cash Book

Receipts £ p	Date	Details	Voucher Number	Total Payments £ p	VAT £ p	£ p	£ p	£ p	£ p	£ p	£ p

Note: the analyis column headings should be completed as required by each exercise.

Chapter 11 resources

CASH IN HAND FORM			
Date		Quantity	Total
Notes	£10		
	£5		
Coins	£2		
	£1		
	50p		
	20p		
	10p		
	5p		
	2p		
	1p		
Total			£

PETTY CASH REIMBURSEMENT REQUEST

Please arrange for a cheque for £ _____ to restore imprest.

Signed _____ Petty Cashier

index

322

for your notes

for your notes

for your notes

for your notes

for your notes

for your notes

for your notes

for your notes

330

for your notes